VALUES AND CONDUCT

VALUES AND CONDUCT

---•❖•---

JOSEPH MARGOLIS

CLARENDON PRESS   OXFORD
OXFORD UNIVERSITY PRESS   NEW YORK
1971

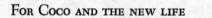
FOR COCO AND THE NEW LIFE

Preface

I HAVE BEEN STRUCK, in composing the account that follows, with two things in particular: first, that the relationship between explanatory theories and the data they are to explain is a puzzle that pervades—in ways that may be significantly different—all the domains of philosophical investigation; and second, that although philosophy does not address itself to all the concerns of the whole man, it addresses the whole man—nowhere more plainly than where personal values are at stake. I find, rather gratifyingly therefore, that the present inquiry leads on to more fundamental questions and, at the same time, affects my own involvement in the affairs of men. But that, frankly, is what I had both hoped and expected.

The essay itself has been distilled (if that is a fair image) from a great many trial efforts, in published papers and invited lectures; it has, consequently, been favored with a good deal of piecemeal criticism as it developed. I am grateful, in particular, to the following journals for permission to incorporate, in variously reshaped ways, material that had originally appeared in them:

The Journal of Philosophy, LXVII, No. 7, April 9, 1970: "Puzzles about Explanation by Reasons and Explanation by Causes"

Ethics, LXXX, No. 1, October, 1969: "Human Acts and Moral Judgments"

American Philosophical Quarterly, VII, No. 3, July 1970: "Ego-
ism and the Confirmation of Metamoral Theories"
The Journal of Value Inquiry, II, No. 1, Spring 1968: "The
Use and Syntax of Value Judgments"
The Journal of Value Inquiry, I, Nos. 3–4, Winter 1967–68:
"Value Judgments and Value Predicates"
The Philosophical Forum, II, No. 3, Spring 1971: " 'Ought'
Implies 'Can' "
The Australasian Journal of Philosophy, XLVIII, No. 1, May
1970: "The Analysis of 'Ought' "
The Australasian Journal of Philosophy, XLV, August 1966:
"Mill's Utilitarianism Again"
Philosophy and Phenomenological Research, XXIII, March
1963: " 'Lying is wrong' and 'Lying is not always wrong.' "

Permission has also been granted, by *The Philosophical Review*, to quote two short passages from John Rawls' "Two
Concepts of Rules," LXIV (1955), 3–22.

And I am grateful to a necessarily more anonymous benefactor
who contributed in a running debate moving at least among the
following schools: Temple University, University of Kansas,
University of Virginia, Kenyon College, Pennsylvania State
University, Washington University.

Finally, I owe a special debt to Mrs. Grace Stuart, Secretary
of the Philosophy Department, Temple University, who, quite
literally, rendered the manuscript legible, not only for possible
readers but also for an actual author; and to Dean George W.
Johnson, of the College of Liberal Arts, and Professor John J.
Fisher, Chairman of the Philosophy Department, both of Temple, who endorsed the enterprise and made the necessary technical assistance possible.

J. M.
December 1970
Philadelphia, Pennsylvania

Contents

VALUES AND CONDUCT

Introduction

As I WRITE, a radical critic of the American liberal tradition is reported in the press to have advanced the view that the constitutional guarantee of free speech should be denied to all those who advocate war, racism, exploitation, and brutality. There is no reason to think that, if the report is accurate, he did not speak with sincerity and moral conviction.

Instances of a similar and even more extreme sort abound today. Perhaps this has always been true. But in our own time the most extraordinarily divergent views have been advocated in the name of morality, humanity, and rationality by individuals and groups of such public prominence and importance that it is not possible to attribute apparent deviation and nonconformity merely to lunatic or unserious or irresponsible or marginal spirits. I take this diversity of conviction to be a fundamental datum for moral theorizing, admittedly unsettling but, more important, largely ignored by relatively comfortable moral theorists in the Western world, even in our own day. Again, militant blacks in the United States, assuming the deep corruption of white society, are preparing, in good conscience, to disrupt and tear down, by the most violent means if necessary and if possible, established educational, business, religious, political, and social institutions that, to their mind, exclude and abuse them. In a sense, students in their attack on the universities and even—if imagination may be stimulated a little—black Africans and the mainland Chinese, are persuaded that disruption and violence may well be the only rational means available, under the various circumstances in which they find themselves, to move the world effectively closer to that vision of a better life to which they devote themselves. Moreover, the visions of all the important communities of the world may hardly be said to converge, once we free ourselves from the illusions of slogans.

There is, as I see it, no single, non-analytic moral thesis that is not contestable, and is not being contested, by serious men. If you say every man should count as one, it will be said that indoctrination and the evils of selected societies vitiate any consensus, that these evils are to be undermined and overthrown at any cost, and that it is always defensible to sacrifice the lives of even extremely large fractions of the population of the world in the name of certain preferred visions. If you hold that certain procedural rules of fairness and justice and equity should be supported for all men, it will be pointed out that these are meaningless outside the context of quite particular societies, that such procedures cannot be separated from substantive disputes respecting the organization and direction of such societies, and that, quite characteristically, such procedures are themselves devices for rationalizing injustice and inequity with respect to populations both inside and outside the preferred community. And if the disputes move on to obviously substantive issues respecting the distribution of property and power, the defense of war and the uses of social energies, the sanctity of life and the right of suicide, the responsibility of men for themselves, their immediate families, their communities, and mankind at large, even the significance and legitimate goals of personal life, it will be entirely clear that there is no agreement in the world today and not much prospect of it.

I will not say that I draw conclusions from these alleged facts, with regard to moral philosophy. On the contrary, I interpret them in accord with certain theories that I favor—that I hope to support in a more acceptable manner. But my view is, quite frankly, that there are no contingent moral truths that are open to discovery in any sense comparable to, say, perceptual discoveries respecting the details of the world—regardless of the conceptual difficulties that may plague claims about the latter; that, given the diversity of moral convictions on every issue, men are, and cannot help being, moral partisans; and that, consequently, to speak of particular persons or doctrines as moral or humane or rational is to risk saying nothing that is demonstrably true, except to those already committed to certain favored partisan teachings.

If what I have just claimed is so, then of course it is extremely difficult to pursue moral philosophy. And this, for at least two intimately related reasons. For one, I, as everyone else, will be inclined to draw for my illustrations of morally relevant data instances that accord with my own convictions. Unless I could suppose—what I am expressly denying—that these may be safely assumed to capture what is true respecting morally significant alternatives of judgment and conduct, I should inevitably be exhibiting the coherence of my general theories for the data I admit rather than testing, in any assignably independent sense, the theories I hold. For another, the traditional theories of moral philosophy respecting relevant issues will not, in principle, bear a relationship to the data to be accounted for that may be found, by way of analogy, among scientific theories and the perceptual data they seek to explain. This is a vexed matter but a crucial one. For, unless one may defend the thesis that, in some sense or other, we may discover what is right and wrong, what good and bad, what ought to be done and what not, we shall never free ourselves from an elaborately question-begging inquiry when we theorize regarding alleged moral data somehow posited as true independently of the partisan theories we subscribe to.

And yet, we suppose that moral philosophy is possible. It used to be thought, rather early in our century, that the trouble with ethical theories was that they sought to support ethically significant alternatives. Fine, advocates of so-called metaethical investigation concluded, we shall avoid such unjustified involvement by sorting out (by restricting ourselves to sorting out) the meaning of ethical terms and by explicating the rules of ethical debate and engagement. Unfortunately, as I hope to show, the thesis that metaethics is not itself ethically partial was naïve and hardly alive to the complexity of ethical disputes. I do not say that this must always be so (that metaethics can never be impartial), but I am prepared to hold that wherever metaethical (and other relatively theoretical) findings do have substantive ethical import, the relevant inquiries may be shown to fail to appreciate the logically close connection between theory and data in the moral domain. Metaethical and related inquiries may be pursued, but to the extent to which they are open to confirmation, they will not, in my opinion, affect alternative moral policies, except (which is important) in the sense of exposing some conceptual weakness (as of inconsistency or indefensibility or appeal to *ad hoc* solutions or the like) of given alternatives. This is, therefore, to acknowledge both that moral theories may, in some range of dispute, be objectively confirmed and still affect conduct and judgment and that substantive moral theories and moral data are related to one another in such a way that we cannot, in any sense analogous with practice in the sciences, attempt to fit competing theories to the admitted data. Put more affirmatively, the fundamental issue behind moral speculation is the explanation of the relationship between the two and its bearing on moral decision and judgment.

There must, correspondingly, be a sense in which 'moral,' 'ethical,' and cognate terms are used relatively neutrally to the partisan doctrines to which we severally subscribe: that is the sense, very simply, in which particular judgments, actions, decisions, policies, principles, rules, and the like are admitted primarily as specimens of the kind of item about which we wish to theorize. From this point of view, Nazis as well as Communists, Christians as well as Buddhists, vegetarians as well as Social Darwinians, egoists as well as altruists may, provisionally, be said to make morally significant decisions and to hold morally significant policies—not only in the sense that their behavior and views may be judged by others but also in the sense in which they themselves provide instances of what it is to make a moral judgment or decision or the like.

I take it as a fair reading of 'moral'—in the categorical sense here intended, as opposed to any doctrinally partisan sense that we are bound to embrace (at least implicitly) in living our lives as we do and in the age in which we do—that any judgment or decision or policy is morally significant if it is concerned with the treatment of any form of life, but primarily human, in terms of relations, conditions, and the like that are thought, by the agents involved, to be preferable over all alternatives, for all living creatures considered. By this construction, I wish to admit, without exaggerating, the possibility of ethical questions concerning at least lower animal life (or plant life or even the inanimate world, should anyone be ingenious enough to justify such an extension) as well as the possibility of ethical questions concerning extra-human or extra-terrestrial life (should the exploration of outer space, if not science fiction, justify the extension). Also by this construction, I wish to emphasize that moral considerations are, by definition, overriding considerations, that wherever we attend to what is suitable or preferred for any living creature *qua* living creature, within a recognized world of such creatures (with whatever forms of membership and organization), we are attending to morally significant issues. Also, with our definition, it is indifferent, as far as merely qualifying as a specimen item, whether one makes an exception of oneself or regards one particular group as privileged or fails to consider the bearing of policies and decisions on the whole range of life; these considerations may, however, properly bear on moral appraisal and, given our previous admissions, on quite variable appraisals. The scope and relative arbitrariness of one's moral commitments could hardly be seriously assessed unless it were admitted that what is being assessed are themselves morally significant items; also, it is itself a substantive issue to decide what the proper and defensible scope of moral concern may be said to be—particularly under the condition that, very often, there is no remotely simple connection between the handling of particular cases and humanity at large. Also by our construction, it is indifferent, again as far as qualifying as a specimen item, whether what the agents believe to be true regarding moral alternatives is or is not true, or whether, genuinely believing what they believe, they act and conduct themselves in ways that may be said to be or not be consistent with their beliefs. For, what the sense is in which moral judgments may be true and false is itself a critical issue for moral philosophy to decide; and the consistency of belief and conduct is itself a substantive question for moral appraisal.

But then, given the categorical sense of 'moral,' there must be a sense in which rational agents have, or are in the process of developing, a moral point of view. That is, if moral considerations are overriding considerations bearing on the conduct of one's own life and the lives of others as such, then to be said to give direction to one's life, in any sense rational, one must consider what values are to be regarded as taking precedence over all alternative values. This, I think, is the meaning, the entirely intelligible meaning, of Immanuel Kant's insistence on treating man "as an end and not as a means only." [1] It is part of rational reflection that we at least raise the question of overriding values for our own and other lives; though, going against Kant's sanguine hopes about the coextensiveness of morality and rationality (by which Kant meant to commit us to quite substantive moral doctrines), we cannot derive any particular moral thesis from this concern: very simply put, men may well be rational in rejecting the deepest moral convictions of one another, so long as they consider the question and decide, for relatively systematic and coherent reasons, to subscribe to these values rather than to those. In short, one cannot be entirely a rational agent if he does not consider how all the conditional commitments he makes—medical, financial, prudential, technical, strategic, and the like—

bear on his commitment to the overriding values of his life. 'Rational' may, conceivably, be coextensive with 'moral,' in the categorical sense of 'moral,' but most certainly not with 'moral' in any partisan or doctrinal sense. To admit otherwise would simply be to fall victim to precisely the sort of conceptual naïveté I have been trying to identify. Also, if we lacked the categorical sense of 'moral,' we should have to invent it, for a rationality sufficiently developed to consider all of the parameters of means-ends relationships and to choose with respect to these is bound to be addressed also to the preference of particular and general goals for "the examined life" as such. The irony is, as I shall attempt to show, that the defensibility of commitments respecting these two sorts of questions is of an entirely different nature and that the less fundamental is, significantly, in a logically more favorable position than the other.

I am impressed, let me say, with what I take to be the need for a radical, revolutionary reorientation of planetary life and with the incredible competition that is going on to share in the direction of it. I find that I am a partisan of quite particular values, but I cannot see how to prove that the values I hold (or that anyone holds) are the true or correct or proper values to hold. Consequently, surprising though it may be, I find that, although it is informed by my particular sympathies, my theorizing does not presuppose my particular values. This means that, in order to hold that the philosophical theories I wish to advance are true, I shall have to construe the relationship between allegedly moral data and allegedly independent theories to be tested with respect to these in a novel way. In fact, I shall construe the theories I advance as accommodating specimen moral views, taken in the categorical sense of 'moral' rather than in the partisan sense; and I shall take care to respect the variety of partisan views that may be possible vis-a-vis the issue at stake. Thus, for instance, it may be feasible to provide a philosophical analysis of 'ought' in its relevant uses in moral discourse, without supposing—for example, with respect to an egoistic thesis—that 'ought'-judgments are not eliminable in any conceivable moral system. Furthermore, I shall suppose that so-called metaethical theories (for example, imperativism) may, though admittedly they need not, harbor partisan ethical convictions of precisely the same sort implied or exhibited by the data alleged to be accounted for by the theories in question. And I shall suppose, for reasons to be supplied, that all large theories such as utilitarianism, deontology, egoism—what I call metamoral theories—are inseparably bound to the preference of partisan moral judgments and decisions and cannot, in principle, be tested with respect to these latter, ordinarily construed as independently posited. In a word, the theories I shall advance I shall suppose to be testable, in a non-partisan sense, with regard to specimen judgments, actions, metamoral principles, and the like, always acknowledging the variability of partisan commitment. Hence, the data are to include, precisely, not only specimen judgments and decisions previous theories have considered—though construed now in a non-partisan way—but also the various theories themselves formulated about these, metaethical and metamoral, insofar as they betray ethical convictions and actually affect (once adopted) subsequent judgment and conduct. But I should not deny that this distinction merely postpones, without resolving, the question of the moral implications of actually using morally significant language.[2]

Seen from this point of view, the conceptual sweep of moral philosophy is quite clear. It must explicate the logical nature of value judgments in a way that is entirely neutral to cognitive claims respecting normative values: here, it engages so-called metaethical issues. It must also, then, resolve the question of moral cognition itself, on the answer to which obviously depends the very tenability of construing moral data in the manner here proposed; for, if some form of cognitivism were defensible, then a full-blown analogy might well be formulated as holding between moral (metamoral) theories and scientific theories; and, in that case, the kind of non-partisanship advocated would be otiose. By parity of reasoning, the untenability of cognitivism would strengthen the interpretation of the prospects of moral philosophy already suggested and, consequently, the force of supportable theories of the kind to be considered. But the question of moral cognition is not so much a metaethical issue as an issue concerning the limits of knowledge: we may justifiably expect some coherent connection between defensible metaethical accounts of moral judgments and whatever may be said about the prospects of moral cognition, but we cannot expect to derive theorems of the one sort from theories of the other. Finally, moral philosophy must explicate the relationships that may hold between relatively institutionalized moral convictions—as expressed in judgments, actions, metamoral principles, and the like—and would-be ethical reform and variable or deviant ethical convictions. This issue, in an obvious sense, is not even admissible, without serious distortion, in a context in which conventional ethical convictions are simply and naïvely taken as settled; for, proposed changes or nonconformity must thereupon be construed as departures from, or as a failure to recognize, moral truths already established. The trouble is that, quite apart from technical questions respecting cognitivism, the history of man testifies to quite radical alterations, through the ages, in acceptable ethical principles as well as significant and serious departures from whatever, in any given age, has been generally accepted as a valid moral principle. The mere admission of the issue, as well as the relevant historical data, while not logically conclusive, raises serious difficulties for a conceptual approach different from the one here proposed. For, on the face of it, cognitivism of any sort would be rather hard-pressed to account satisfactorily for this set of data; and, on the other, their admission raises difficulties for any would-be (metamoral) theory alleged to fit the relatively independent facts of moral practice. But speculation here must be careful not to legislate, in a morally partisan sense, what the appropriate or acceptable way might be, in which reform or deviation must be linked with prevailing ethical values; here, the best way to proceed seems to be that of drawing analogies to other contexts in which values exhibit relative variability—for instance, as in connoisseurship in the arts and in variations in taste. The principal questions here concern the relationship between conduct and the adoption of putatively normative values.

What stands out, then, is the coherence of these overarching moral theories designed to fit the wide range of data already mentioned. The data themselves may be interpreted in a variety of ways, but disputes may be raised piecemeal at certain strategic foci of discussion and the tenability of otherwise global theories will be seriously affected. Justify cognitivism and an enormous run of competing theories are at once ruled out of court; defeat it and speculation must move in relatively unpopular ways. I have noted also, in relevant philosophical disputes, that crucial judgments often are admitted as true, without a murmur—when it is plain that to do so is tantamount to disqualifying particular theories and that to subscribe to these theories entails rejecting the judgments in question. Thus, for instance, to admit that one genuinely has obligations is, as I shall argue, incompatible with holding an egoistic principle. What baffles the naïve egoist and comforts his equally naïve opponent is the assumption that, independently of their dispute, it can be decisively established—and not merely by joint consent—that one genuinely has obligations. Here, we may see that we are actually faced with systematic considerations bearing on the tenability of cognitivism and the extent to which egoism would require a reinterpretation of conventional obligations. The point is that the tenability of a large moral theory of the sort at issue depends on a great many appraisals of comprehensive scope, arbitrariness, internal coherence, accommodation and adjustment of standard runs of cases, and the like—even without presuming that there are relatively hard data in the moral domain corresponding, by fair analogy, with the perceptual data on which science depends.

What is fascinating to observe is the way in which the seemingly abstract disputes of moral philosophy actually come to bear on the rational pursuit of moral issues. For not only is it rational, as I have argued—given that we reason regarding conditional and transient goals, in terms of the efficiency and coordination of means and ends—to determine the overriding goals of life, it is rational also to attempt to formulate these consistently with the most coherent and comprehensive picture of the world in which we find ourselves. This is perhaps the chief point of construing moral philosophy as we have. For, if one takes the moral domain as a distinct and relatively separate domain of inquiry, it is well-nigh impossible to avoid accepting venerable moral judgments and decisions, warmly applauded or authoritatively admitted by influential figures, to constitute a body of hard data with which moral theory must begin. To place the signal questions of moral theory in the setting of all our speculations about the world is to provide most reliably for the avoidance of otherwise attractive but indefensible doctrines. And yet, to do so is also, given the difficulty of defending substantive theories, to dramatize the incredibly delicate position of a rational agent: for, since he cannot avoid committing himself to overriding values or exploring the specific defensibility and conceptual coherence of his choices, he cannot really avoid the philosophical investigations here sketched. And, of course, to appreciate the tenuous grounds on which the firmest and dearest moral convictions rest is to appreciate the extraordinary implications of moral severity, moral confidence, and moral responsibility.

There are also, I must say, fair grounds for the suspicion that moral philosophy is fatuous, however irresistible. When I consider the matter in terms of personal conviction, I find that I am pretty well bound to speculate about realistic changes that I find desirable in terms of the institutions of my own country (usually the most local) but that the matters of gravest importance to me concern what can only be called planetary matters. The result is that I oscillate between fairly restricted projects that have a debatable chance of being realized and visionary goals that seem little more than clichés. Still, it is not merely that questions of practicality are more readily settled at home than abroad—in any case, this is not always so; it is rather that the important moral issues respecting life and death, disease and hunger, war and peace, education, shelter, the uses of men's careers, and the like are extraordinarily complicated and defy the kind of easy classification, misleadingly encouraged by minor (though manageable) textbook cases, that suggest the adequacy of straightforward rules and principles. Here again, however, the issue may be raised afresh and made to yield theorems respecting moral classification, judgment, rules, and principles that, though primarily metaethical in nature, nevertheless influence, in a manner already suggested, morally relevant conduct itself. And if such may be formulated, the limitations mentioned may be said to affect social engineering rather more than moral philosophy.

Finally, it may be supposed that, contrary to my initial warnings, I have construed moral theories as intended to fit relatively independently confirmed data. In a way, this is true; and in a way, not. For, although one cannot (meaningfully) hope to confirm a theory unless it is a theory about some body of data and confirmable with respect to it, I wish to hold that moral theories traditionally thought to be thus confirmable are not actually separable from the alleged data they are to account for. The adjustment required by this consideration is substantial. The traditional theories are themselves normative theories, that is, theories that presuppose or claim to establish overriding (or, normative) moral values. Moral judgments themselves concern precisely such values; and if one subscribes to certain judgments of this sort, one is inevitably bound to subscribe also to some set of principles or theories compatible with these. But the data to be accommodated by the theories to be hereafter proposed include both judgments and these traditional (metamoral)

theories, now construed as mere specimens of moral conviction
—in the categorical sense of 'moral'—and without the assumption of actual normative force. That is, the traditional theories
are avowedly normative in intent; whereas, by a simple adjustment, I shall consider them and specimen judgments as merely
putatively normative. My fundamental question, therefore, is
not, What values ought to be, or are, the true, overriding values
for human beings? but rather, Given that men subscribe to
such-and-such overriding values and defend them and reason
about them in thus-and-such ways, what are the logical properties of moral judgments and in what sense can they be or not
be confirmed? It is clear, I think, that, if some form of cognitivism can be supported, the two questions may be collapsed;
and if, on the other hand, cognitivism can be defeated, they will
equally significantly diverge. But this is merely to say again
that we shall have to assess the over-all coherence of competing
theories and that, in the special circumstance in which cognitivism proves to be a true theory, to be a rational moral partisan
is to be a partisan of true moral values. Also, it is to admit that
it is extremely difficult to be certain that the theories we advance
as thoroughly non-partisan are not, in fact, partisan doctrines
in masquerade; for it is difficult, though not impossible, to distinguish partisan conclusions from those non-partisan conclusions that set conceptual limits to competing doctrines. But
this is simply one of the natural difficulties of the inquiry.

PART ONE

PART ONE

CHAPTER I

Value Judgments and Value Predicates

THERE ARE TWO fundamental issues bearing, narrowly, on moral philosophy and, more widely, on value theory that, since the appearance of G. E. Moore's *Principia Ethica*,[1] have been more or less confused one with the other. One is the issue of the objectivity of value judgments, that is, the issue of admissible grounds for the public confirmation of value judgments; and the other is the issue of the so-called Naturalistic Fallacy, that is, the issue of the differences among predicates like 'good' and 'yellow.' I have in fact, in formulating the two issues, already sketched their signal logical distinction. For, the issue of objectivity concerns *judgments* and the issue of the Fallacy concerns *predicates*. Very much hangs on this. A glance at the history of metaethics shows at once that, as with A. J. Ayer,[2] C. L. Stevenson,[3] and R. M. Hare,[4] the rejection of Moore's non-naturalistic account of 'good' goes hand-in-hand with serious doubts about the objectivity of moral judgments; and the recent recovery of the objectivity of moral judgments, most prominent perhaps in a variety of utilitarian doctrines, suggests and even at times celebrates the fallacy of the Naturalistic Fallacy.

The importance of these two matters lies, very simply, in their strategic position in any comprehensive scanning of truth claims possible in the moral domain and other domains of value. Nevertheless, it is quite possible to exaggerate this importance; for the issues mentioned concern only the logical features of certain judgments and certain predicates and leave relatively untouched whatever may be questioned regarding our putative knowledge of values as such. The restriction promises a certain economy inasmuch as, according to the thesis to be advanced, value judgments in all domains of interest exhibit the logical properties of two basic, alternative sorts. Furthermore, the signal differences among value judgments discriminated as medical, legal, moral, aesthetic, and the like, have—apart from differences bearing on the relationship between judgment and conduct—more to do with the grounds on which particular sets of values are posited than with the logical differences to be considered. Consequently, it will be very useful to isolate, at the very start, the formal features of value judgments and then to complicate, in the appropriate way, the account of the actual setting in which these several kinds of judgments are used—with an eye both to cognitive issues and to issues regarding relations between judgment and conduct. The result is that conclusions drawn in the present setting must be construed in a correspondingly restricted way: in particular, to speak, as I shall, about certain value judgments as factual judgments is to speak, provisionally, of no more than of certain formal similarities. We should otherwise be running ahead of our evidence.

Relevant disputes in the context of value theory prove, unfortunately, to be rather easily misdirected by the admission of certain otherwise entirely relevant considerations. Thus, for instance, the admission of the *de gustibus* principle tends to unnerve the advocates of objectivity. The reason is that theorists who address themselves to value judgments tend, in what might usefully be labeled a Kantian spirit, to generalize about value judgments as though they all belonged to the same logical bundle. This attitude often manifests itself in an accurately Kantian voice, in the view that not only are moral and aesthetic value judgments of logically different kinds, but also specimens of each kind exhibit uniform logical properties.[5] I shall suggest, in this regard, that every domain of value judgments—whether moral or aesthetic or medical or legal—contains judgments of logically mixed kinds and that the distinct kinds of such judgments are not confined in any particular such domain.

On the other hand, attention to the motives for issuing, and the ulterior uses of, value judgments—for example, the characteristically action-guiding function of moral judgments—raises doubts about the declarative form of such judgments and, hence, about the possibility of treating them as open to confirmation of any kind. These various uses need not be denied and have, of course, their relevance in an account of the logical properties of value judgments. But I shall argue that it is also a function of value judgments (not of all value judgments, as we shall see) to be used to declare what is the case. Here, the long-standing controversy about facts and values, marked classically in David Hume's notice of the roles of 'is' and 'ought,' inevitably arises.[6] Hume, I suggest, placed the emphasis wrongly on the copula, whereas it should be placed on the predicates of the relevant judgments. In short, the distinction between facts and values may be fully clarified by distinguishing among predicates and not by contrasting judgment and persuasion (or something of the sort).

But I must make my claims good.

There are, as I see it, two distinct kinds of value judgments that we make, discriminable without regard to the motives for their issue or the ulterior uses to which they may be put. I call these *findings* and *appreciative judgments*. I admit that the same sentences, that is, the same strings of words, may, sometimes, be used both as findings and as appreciative judgments; and I admit that some judgments in actual use exhibit properties of both of these kinds. I shall offer supporting illustrations once we are clear about the critical distinctions.

Findings, insofar as they are judgments, behave in precisely the same way as factual judgments, that is, there are recognizably public grounds on which to test the truth of findings; logically contrary judgments cannot both be true, and judgments confirmed as true state what is the case. *Given* the logical properties of factual judgments, it cannot be shown that findings, insofar as they are judgments, are distinguishable from factual judgments. Disputes about specimen instances of both act in identical ways (though this is not to say that the kinds of evidence bearing on different factual judgments may not exhibit important logical differences and may not have differentially important consequences).

It is, for instance, a medical finding that Peter has cancer; and it is a legal finding that John murdered Mary; and it is a finding proper to the orchard industry that the winesaps from a particular grove of trees are predominantly fancy. It is *pointless,* on considerations of testing alone, to dispute whether such judgments are or are not value judgments. We may of course notice that cancer entails a loss of health, that murder is essentially reprehensible, that fancy apples are labeled in accord with certain prevailing preferences. Nevertheless, these considerations do not bear at all on the *testing* of the relevant judgments. We have only to be clear about the criteria or tests or paradigms of the conditions in question to be able to determine, on the presentation of the relevant discriminable features of things, whether Peter has cancer, whether John murdered Mary, whether these winesaps are fancy. Doubts about the precision and conclusiveness of such testing, no matter how legitimate, apply equally to factual judgments and to findings and will, on inspection, offer not the slightest basis for distinguishing between the two. We determine, in very similar ways, whether Paul has sickle-cell anemia and what his red blood corpuscle count is; and we determine, in very similar ways, whether John murdered Mary and whether John had dinner with Mary; and we determine, in very similar ways, whether these winesaps are fancy and whether their skins are uniformly smooth. Considerations of these sorts strengthen the claim that, *if* we wish to distinguish between factual judgments and findings, we shall have to do so on the basis of the kinds of *predicates* involved and not on the basis of the ways in which their truth and falsity may be assessed.

Simple as the foregoing considerations are, they show at a stroke that the traditional puzzle (mnemonically linked with Hume) about the transition from factual judgments to value judgments has been rather badly mismanaged. For, so the argument would go, in a *given conceptual framework,* in a framework in which, say, the concepts of red blood corpuscle count and sickle-cell anemia were in use, it *would* be possible to move, in an argument, from factual judgments to value judgments without a merely logical blunder occurring. So also, one would be able, as in judgments of murder, to move from what is the case to what one ought or ought not to do. Undoubtedly, important questions arise even here—for instance, about the proper construction of the word 'ought' in moral and legal judgments —but these call for refinements (some of which we shall return to) that do not threaten the main issue. On the basis of appeal to public procedures for testing the truth and falsity of claims and judgments, there is absolutely no distinction that can be advanced that would allow us to sort out factual judgments proper from those value judgments that I am calling findings. And, if this is so, then, as I wish to demonstrate, there is far more difference, in logically important respects, between the two sorts of value judgments initially mentioned than there is between factual judgments and at least one class of value judgments.

Consider now an illustration of the second sort of value judgment, what I have called appreciative judgments. Let me be clear about my use of terms here. I do *not* wish to hold that all questions of *appreciation* involve valuational distinctions of some sort. There is an obvious sense in which, as a medical student, I may appreciate, by careful attention, the technical complexities of a certain surgical operation: I may, so to say, merely appreciate the relevant facts for what they are. But when I speak of appreciative judgments I mean to speak of placing a value on things because of the way—still to be detailed—in which we appreciate them. I have in mind the following sort of case. If I judge a woman to be lovely, I will so judge her, normally, because of my own personal taste. What my taste is will concern a special range of facts about me—for instance, my attitudes, sensations, and feelings of pleasure, pain, attraction, indifference, preference, repulsion, parts of my behavior including verbal behavior that are taken to manifest my taste in terms of likes and dislikes. Now, if I issue an appreciative judgment—that Lily is lovely—I shall have issued a value judgment that, logically, presupposes my taste's being what it is. I regard it as a defining characteristic of an appreciative judgment that the proper range of use of the value predicate employed be compatible with a certain range of taste. So, for instance, if I say that Lily is lovely and secretly detest her (that is, have feelings that would not be appropriate in sincerely predicating loveliness of Lily) then either I have made a verbal mistake of some sort or else I have not issued an appreciative judgment (as not being a judgment at all but, rather, a piece of spite and irony; or, as being a judgment of another sort, depending on *your* taste rather than mine). Under these circumstances, my taste *cannot serve as a supporting reason for my judgment,* though to construe the judgment as an appreciative judgment is to presuppose a certain commensurate taste on my part and though, within limits, what my taste is may be determined as a matter of fact.

This much of the account already provides the crucial difference between findings and appreciative judgments. For findings do not presuppose, or logically depend on, taste (or, more generally, personal conviction), and appreciative judgments do. Consider that I judge Lily to be lovely and that you deny it. If the judgment were construed as a finding, then at least one of us would be wrong. But if the judgment were an appreciative judgment, then, precisely because our tastes differed and because the judgments presupposed such a difference, our judgments could not properly be taken to be contraries. The important point is not that they would not be contraries (or even contradictories) but that they are or are not taken as contraries on the strength of their being either findings or appreciative judgments. That John murdered Mary and that John did not murder Mary *are* incompatible judgments and, as such, must be findings rather than appreciative judgments. (I do not mean to deny here that 'murder' may also be used in an appreciative sense, as when one says, figuratively, that the coal mines murder the countryside.) There are value judgments that may be paired as contraries or contradictories; and all such must be findings. And there are value judgments that, *if they were construed as findings,* would be paired as contraries or contradictories; but all such, as not so construed, must be appreciative judgments.

What we shall have to go on to consider—what is regularly missed, for instance, in the emotivist and imperativist views— is that *even appreciative judgments may be defended and attacked in their own logically appropriate way,* that merely to dismiss apparent conflicts of judgment is not to dismiss differences in judgment. But this issue will have to rest for a moment. What we have managed to do thus far is to contrast findings and appreciative judgments in at least two logically critical respects. For one thing, findings do not presuppose appropriate taste on the part of the judge, and appreciative judgments do. And for another, would-be findings may be paired as contraries or contradictories and, in the same sense, appreciative judgments may not.

A word of clarification is due here. I may judge that Lily is lovely, ignoring my own taste, by considering her in the light of *your taste.* If your taste is sufficiently stable and regular, and if your appreciative criteria may be formulated, then *my* judgment may either be construed as a finding *relative* to your taste or I may be supposed to have made an appreciative judgment in *your place.* Since the matter is slight, we are likely to prefer the second way of speaking; but, in principle, the first way of speaking is very much like the way in which we speak of fancy apples. *If* I presuppose the prevailing tastes of the community, as in fashion and in food, the judgments I render—which do not presuppose my own taste or anyone else's taste in particular (however it may or may not conform to prevailing taste)—will count as findings.[7] This suggests the historical continuity, as distinct from the question of logical resemblance, between findings and appreciative judgments. Again, I may judge Lily to be lovely on one occasion and not on another, and even to judge her to be lovely for certain reasons and to judge her not to be lovely for precisely those features that I had considered in offering my previous reasons. I should not have contradicted myself, though I should have exhibited fickle taste. Here, we see that *unless* one's taste may be counted on to have some measure of regularity, we should lose interest in construing appreciative judgments as *judgments,* as calling for some sort of appropriate support; we should then emphasize, what would normally have been only presupposed by such judgments, that our speaker was *manifesting* or *exhibiting* or *expressing* or *reporting* his taste—rather like clapping at a performance or saying candidly, "That's very good." The reason would-be appreciative judgments degenerate into expressions of taste is, precisely, that we cannot properly marshall the defending reasons for the judgment and are obliged to fall back on consulting *what the taste is.* And the reason would-be appreciative judgments may be raised to the status of findings is, precisely, that though considerations of taste may still obtain, such considerations no longer have any autobiographical import. Distinctions of this kind, it may be mentioned, are not countenanced by emotivism.

To return to the main argument, I wish to draw attention to a third, decisive difference between findings and appreciative judgments. In all the ways that are open to factual judgments, findings make predications of things. We are called on, in assessing findings, to determine straight-forwardly whether what is affirmed is the case. If I claim that Peter has cancer, that John murdered Mary, that these winesaps are fancy apples, you will test, in whatever sense the question is allowed for matters of fact, whether what I claim is so. On the other hand, because incompatible judgments cannot arise in the same sense for appreciative judgments as for findings, you cannot, in assessing my claim, determine straightforwardly whether or not what I claim is so. It is easy, but incorrect, to conclude from this that my claim cannot, in any sense, be defended or attacked. What is important to grasp is what, open to challenge with respect to findings, cannot be provided a parallel among appreciative judgments; and what, open to challenge with respect to appreciative judgments, is precluded from findings.

I have reference, in the first place, to the fact that the familiar distinction between what is the case and what merely appears to be the case but is not, holds for findings but not for appreciative judgments. John may have appeared to murder Mary but may not actually have done so. It cannot be the case that Lily only appears to be lovely but is not, or is lovely though she appears not to be. For, if it is the case that she either *is* or *is not* lovely, you will be asserting something incompatible if you assert that she is not or is lovely. To hold that appreciative judgments cannot be paired as contraries or contradictories entails that the 'is'-'appears' contrast must be rejected. Alternatively put, if the contrast is retained, it will have to serve some altogether different use from that which marks out, for findings and factual judgments, what actually is the case from what we may merely believe to be the case. It may, for instance, serve to mark the prejudice or the authority of our own taste: Lily really is lovely (which you might discern if you only *had* taste!). The second consideration is this: in challenging findings, as factual judgments, we challenge whether what is claimed is the case; but in challenging appreciative judgments, since this is not possible, we challenge only whether what is *said* to be the case is *justifiably so said*. I hope I am understood here. The sense of 'saying' that I have in mind designates a logically weaker way of speaking of things than the way in which we ascribe properties to things that they *may be found to have*. Loveliness, as ascribed to Lily in an appreciative judgment, *is not a property she may or may not have*. It is a property we may *say* she has, *given* the requisite taste on our part. As I have already indicated, these properties gradually, in societies exhibiting relatively stable and uniform taste, acquire the status of being properties that things may *have*—precisely because the relevant considerations of taste are no longer those of autobiographical tastes presupposed in issuing appreciative judgments.

This difference between findings and appreciative judgments may be put somewhat more cleanly. The predicates that are employed in appreciative judgments are applied to things only on the condition of the judge's having a certain commensurate taste (if he judges Lily to be lovely, he must at least have a favorable attitude toward her appearance or manner or the like). He applies the predicate to Lily on the condition that he has such an attitude and would not, if he lacked such an attitude. He *says* that Lily is lovely, consulting her describable features— whether of the sort marked by factual judgments or by findings or by both—*because he puts a certain value on these in accord with his taste*. I may not share his taste and, therefore, may fail to put the same value on her describable features, but I may very well see why, given his taste, he does put such and such a value on Lily. I may see this and I may judge whether or not he is in any sense justified in putting the value he does on Lily; although, if I vindicate *him*, I shall not (not having the same taste) be bound to share his judgment. He may be justified, given his taste, in *saying* that Lily is lovely, but he cannot show, insofar as his taste is decisive, that Lily is lovely.

Obviously, the way in which we challenge appreciative judgments is logically quite weak. Correspondingly, our interest in challenging such judgments is restricted and quite tolerant. We are interested, for example, in challenging the judgments of connoisseurs in the arts, precisely because their tastes may be supposed to be so firm and reliable that we wonder how, as they expand their assessment of a growing range of works, they are able to put values on new items, for admissible reasons, that fit with relative ease into the range of their admitted tastes and corresponding reasons. There is, of course, always the by-benefit to be had as well, that new discriminations are provided that may bear on the revision and adjustment of our own taste. At any rate, the form of challenge appropriate to appreciative judgments is easy enough to mark out. If, in addition to knowing that such predicates as 'lovely' are taste-bound in the manner indicated, we know the kinds of considerations that may properly be drawn on for the ascription of these predicates, we are in a position to assess whether a given appreciative judgment is defensible or not. I may, for example, draw attention to what, in Lily, might count toward declaring her intelligent; I should not then have offered any reason for saying that she is lovely. I may, for example, draw attention to her graciousness and tact —where, rather in the spirit of Aristotle's *Ethics,* prevailing taste has deposited a considerable body of agreed-upon distinctions; but if it is a fact that I am mistaken about these, since the evidence actually points to her enviousness and spite, I should not have justified my judgment. In assessing appreciative judgments, we judge whether what is said, given one's taste, is compatible with the facts and relevantly connected with the sorts of considerations that bear on ascribing the value in question. And in assessing findings, we judge only whether what is claimed to be the case actually is the case. It goes without saying that we often pass appreciative judgments about another's tastes—consulting, as we must, his own range of appreciative judgments and the relative defensibility of them.

It is worth noting, also, that the same sentences may sometimes be used to express findings and appreciative judgments and that some value judgments combine the properties of both findings and appreciative judgments. I may, for example, construe modern warfare as murder, meaning by this that, in spite of the fact that killing another on the battlefield is not regarded in the law as murder, on the strength of my convictions regarding human life, I put that valuational mark upon warfare. I have advanced an appreciative judgment, not a finding—which is of course by no means to devalue the judgment, only to indicate its logical properties. Again, in judging the best of breed at a dog show, preliminary considerations of the relative merits of contenders clearly lead to findings (trainers may even groom their dogs with an eye to mustering points) but the final judgment presupposes appreciative preferences; the same considerations, I might add, apply to the selection of the winners of beauty contests and to the appraisal of diamonds. (I draw attention, incidentally, to the fact that, here I am speaking somewhat more generously of appreciative judgments, in speaking not merely of varying *tastes* but also of varying personal *convictions* and *preferences*. Reference to the fine arts, dogs, and women tends to restrict the appropriate idiom.)

Still, the objectivity of value judgments seems jeopardized by the relativity of values and, in particular, by the fact that even findings may, as in judging fancy apples, depend on the emergence of a certain prevailing taste. The force of these considerations is easily misunderstood. As far as value judgments are concerned, it cannot be denied that such objectivity as they enjoy is relative to a given conceptual framework; but then, precisely the same observation may be made of factual judgments. The relativity of values and the dependence at times on prevailing taste or convictions draw attention rather to the distinction of the *predicates* belonging to the range of value judgments as opposed to factual judgments. *If* given predicates are regarded as value predicates, the corresponding judgments are value judgments; and if they are not so regarded, the corresponding judgments are not value judgments. Of course, all the relevant predicates of appreciative judgments are value predicates, since they are properly ascribed to things on grounds that presuppose our particular tastes or personal convictions. But it is not normally such judgments that raise the most serious quarrels, since, as we have seen, they cannot be confused with factual judgments at all. The serious issue is bound to concern the predicates of findings.

Here, the most illuminating considerations may be drawn from moral and legal disputes. Imagine that John has actually murdered Mary. To determine that he has is to determine certain facts and that his connection with these facts is reprehensible. But, we may well ask, what are the grounds for deciding that what he has done, the sort of thing he has done, should be regarded as a morally or legally reprehensible act? On what grounds can we justify fixing the category of murder in our conceptual framework? Can we, for instance, say that the reprehensibility of taking another's life, in those ways that may be collected as murder, is entailed by the very concept of a human being? *If* we could say so, then we should find it very difficult, if not impossible, to draw a line between factual judgments and value judgments.

I have already argued that we cannot distinguish between factual judgments and findings, as far as questions of evidence and defensibility are concerned. Now, we are in danger of being altogether unable to distinguish between the two, since, if the concept of human nature entails the concept of the reprehensibility of taking another's life in certain ways (among other morally or legally significant consequences), we shall be unable, to that extent, to sort out merely factual predicates from value predicates. But there seems to be no more promising basis for discriminating value judgments and factual judgments than in terms of the logical properties of the judgments themselves or in terms of the logical properties of their appropriate predicates.

We must allow, to come to the issue, that there are runs of predicates that are entirely without valuational import. For example, to classify something as a stone does not presuppose or entail in any sense whatsoever having a concept of goodness relative to being a stone. The concept of a stone, we may say, does not entail the concept of a good stone: stones are classified as such, particular things are judged to be stones, on the strength of their resemblance to admitted specimens of stones —which specimens need not be excellent or preeminent in any respect—and not on the strength of their manifesting certain excellences thought appropriate to stones. That there are such categories is precisely what allows us to mark off factual judgments.

Now, among our classificatory concepts, some behave logically the way the concept of a stone does and some do not. For instance, the concept of a knife entails the concept of a good knife: a knife is defined in terms of its function; and to know its function is to know what would count as relative success and failure with respect to that function. Particular knives may be poor *as* knives, poor *in so far as they are* knives; and an explication of what it means to be a knife will itself provide us with considerations by which to judge the merit of particular objects relative to the function of a knife. But though stones may, on the provision of suitable criteria, be judged to be good or poor stones (whatever the point of such assessment), the provision of even minimal criteria cannot be defended as an explication of the meaning of the concept of a stone.

Consider now that the concept of a postman behaves more like the concept of a knife than like the concept of a stone. Postmen have their function; and to know what it means to be a postman is to know in what ways men may be judged to be good or poor *with regard to being a postman*. A similar argument holds for such human roles as those of policeman, judge, guardian, teacher, husband, realtor, lawyer, priest, and the like. But it is crucial to see that it does not hold for the concepts of a man, a human being, a person, a child, an adult—that is, for concepts that do not directly concern the *roles* or *functions* or *purposes* human beings may serve. To suppose that the concept of a good man, that is, the concept of what it is to be good *qua human being,* can be derived from the concept of a man *is* to suppose that man has an essential function. But the fact is that we can and do classify creatures as men merely on the strength of their resemblance to admissible specimens—indifferently to considerations of human excellence of any sort—and it is not clear in what sense men, apart from the particular functions they may serve, have a distinct function merely as men. Such well-known moral injunctions as those against taking one's life and those favoring the development of one's talents clearly presuppose, as in Kant's or Spinoza's account, an essential purpose inherent in humanity itself. But the difficulty, very simply put, is that man is not an artifact or a particular role that some creature may serve. From this point of view, *whatever* excellences we may assign to men *qua* men, we cannot, for logical reasons, posit such excellences as entailed by the very concept of a man.

Here lies the decisive clue distinguishing values and facts, an alternative way of putting the insight of the Naturalistic Fallacy. What is good for man *qua* man cannot be derived from the concept of a man; and the goodness of everything else, including filling the roles that men may occupy, is whatever it is, relative to specifiable human purposes and interests. Of course, in a sense all concepts are what they are, relative to human purposes and interests; but the measure of merit of things of particular kinds supposes that the kinds themselves have a function or purpose or role assigned by men. The classification of animals may accord with the explanatory purposes of men, but the classification of things *as* knives and postmen is itself a classification with respect to function and purpose. Hence, that value judgments and factual judgments may be indistinguishable with respect to evidence and defensibility is entirely consistent with distinguishing between valuational and factual predicates. Trivially, wherever valuational norms are introduced and judgment concerns assessment relative to these, we have value judgments and not merely factual judgments. The critical matter is not the distinction between the two sorts of judgment but rather this: that the norms cannot be posited as an explication of the concept of a man. This explains for instance the sense in which valuational norms may be culturally variable and yet judgments with respect to these norms may be findings rather than appreciative judgments.

There is another critical advantage to our theory. If valuational and non-valuational predicates are distinguished by reference to their roles in our conceptual theories—in particular, by reference to whether or not their use entails the use of normative considerations—then it is entirely possible to hold at one and the same time that valuational predicates are extensionally equivalent to sets of purely descriptive predicates (that is, non-valuational predicates) and that they are nevertheless distinguishable from such purely descriptive predicates. This means that it is *not* necessary, in providing for the distinction of value judgments, to admit some distinctive use of such judgments—as emotivists and imperativists require; that distinction is sufficiently supported by the conceptual difference between the two sorts of predicates. To take a much-discussed case, if certain conditions of offense (O) are fulfilled, then it cannot consistently be denied that a certain piece of behavior is rude (R); the conditions of O may be extensionally equivalent to those of R, even though "we have here an example of a non-evaluative premiss from which an evaluative conclusion can be deduced." [8] The deduction is justified on the basis of the equivalence; the distinction of the conclusion is justified on the basis of our conception of the predicate involved. But to say this is to say nothing of the cognitive questions at stake or of relevant grounds for rejecting or revising the criteria on which the equivalence rests.[9] That is, one must not confuse linguistic and moral (or other valuational) issues.

I am suggesting that the argument of the Naturalistic Fallacy may be recovered by revision. We may say, first of all, that the distinction between facts and values concerns predicates rather than judgments; secondly, that valuational norms depend on human purposes and interests; thirdly, that we are able to, and do, classify things in non-valuationally significant ways; and finally, that no valuational norms posited for men may be derived from the concept of a man. One way of stressing the distinction of the revised argument is to review Moore's original contrast of the allegedly simple qualities, good and yellow. According to our present view, 'good' cannot be the name of a simple quality, as Moore supposed. This is not to say that sentences of the form 'X is good' are invariably findings or even judgments—they may, for instance be commendations or expressions of taste. But if they are findings, they are elliptically stated: things are good-relative-to-some-purpose (or function) or good-as-of-some-kind or good-with-respect-to-some-role (or office). Colors are what they are, as discriminated under standard conditions, without regard to the nature of the things of which they are colors; but 'goodness' is a complex predicate (or a set of related complex predicates) the analysis of which requires refer· ence to particular kinds of things.

Another feature of the revised argument, barely noted above, is the ease with which the cultural relativity of values is accommodated—what would remain inadmissible on the intuitionist's non-naturalistic account of goodness. For, we have even conceded the sense in which predicates originally employed in appreciative judgments may be raised to the status of employment in findings, on the condition of regularizing the tastes or convictions of a community. But here, of course, we see the relative informality, in the context of values, with which we may come to (or cease to) speak of what *is* the case, having previously (or latterly) restricted ourselves to *putting* a value on things in accord with our tastes. The very prominence of taste, conviction, attitude, preference, and the like in the *evolution* of our value categories is precisely what calls for a reasoned account of the continuity and discontinuity of facts and values.

I find the adequate answer in the distinction between judgments and predicates and the relationship between findings and appreciative judgments.

I should like to emphasize once again, however, the difference between value judgments as such and the ulterior uses to which they may be put—without at all denying that utterances may convey at one and the same time that use of language which is judging and those uses, like persuasion and the direction of action, which are often confused with it. It is very nearly conclusive merely to concede that factual judgments, like value judgments, may also serve such ulterior uses and to concede that it is logically possible to use sentences solely for the purpose of making judgments. Certainly, these considerations disqualify emotivism as an adequate theory of value judgments and seriously weaken imperativism. In fact, imperativism cannot possibly be advanced with any prospect of adequacy outside of the moral and legal domains. The attempt, as, for example, in Stevenson,[10] to combine emotivism and imperativism must fail simply because of the impropriety of directing or commanding anyone to acquire attitudes, emotions, tastes, feelings, and the like, which cannot be deliberately adopted and which, nevertheless, may be appraised; and the fact that there are enormous runs of value judgments both within the moral domain (for example, the judgment that St. Francis lived the life of a saint) and without (for example, judgments about the beauty of things) that cannot remotely be thought to be action-guiding raises grave doubts about the mere relevance of imperativism as a theory about value judgments in general.

Moral 'ought'-judgments are perhaps the last refuge of imperativism and of the resistance to construing findings and factual judgments as much the same, as far as evidence and defensibility are concerned. But even here, our thesis can be effectively maintained. Consider only that to judge that one ought to do X (in the morally or legally relevant sense) is (as a rough approximation) to judge, that one has, or is under, an obligation of some sort: *this* may be construed as a finding, relative to a given conceptual framework. But, more than this, explicate the sense of 'ought' as action-guiding, in the sense that if one acknowledged the propriety of the judgment, it would be inconsistent—to that extent—not to adjust one's conduct accordingly: it would no longer be necessary to construe the judgment in imperativist terms; moral consistency, or consistency between judgment and conduct, would suffice. Finally, admit that *such* a judgment may be action-guiding, in the sense that it is issued *to direct* another with respect to his obligations: this use then becomes an additional, ulterior use to which the judgment has been put; furthermore, it is not a use to which 'ought'-judgments may be put in discourse adjusted for *all three* grammatical persons—we may resolve, but not, say, command ourselves, to act in accord with our obligations. It is easy to see that we may accommodate other such ulterior uses of value judgments—for example, the emotivist use of expressing conviction or feeling.

There appear, then, to be no serious logical difficulties to characterizing findings in much the same way as factual judgments. To do so is not to ignore, or to fall victim to, the Naturalistic Fallacy. But to distinguish between value judgments and factual judgments is to attend to the nature of relevant predicates and not to considerations of defensibility. Furthermore, no theory of the logical uniformity of value judgments will do, for, as we have seen, findings are quite fundamentally different from appreciative judgments. The most prominent theories opposing our own—emotivism and imperativism—fail in a double sense: they construe value judgments as being of a uniform sort; also, they lead to anomalies when generalized, and they render themselves inessential to the extent that they can be defended at all.

CHAPTER 2

The Use and Syntax of Value Judgments

IT IS A VERY DEEPSEATED, but altogether mistaken, practice, in generalizing about value judgments, to suppose that moral judgments or aesthetic judgments or other sorts of similar judgments have logically uniform uses within their respective domains. The practice is, familiarly, Kantian and finds its most recent expression (not entirely in accord with Kant's own preferences) in imperativism and emotivism. But we cannot, if we take a reasonably broad sample of judgments that may be construed as moral or aesthetic judgments or the like, defend a single distinctive and comprehensive model for such a set; and we cannot, if we attempt to mark off the aesthetic and the moral and other such categories from one another, provide for the satisfactory classification of any reasonably broad sample of judgments. Neither do the run of judgments of this or that sort show comfortable uniformities, nor can we say with confidence what the boundaries are between this and that sort of judgment.

Let me illustrate.

It is often held, and prominently by R. M. Hare,[1] that moral judgments are action-guiding, by which is meant that the essential use of moral judgments is to *direct* people with respect to future conduct: this is the heart of imperativism or prescriptivism. Apparent anomalies, initially of a grammatical sort, are obviated by technical enlargements of the competent scope of imperatives. So, for example, suitable past-tense and first-person imperatives are invented or the contexts in which relevant inquiry about oneself or the past arises are interpreted as logically dependent on present- or future-tense and second- or third-person imperatives. The same sort of adjustment may be attempted for fictional, hypothetical, and counterfactual cases. There are, nevertheless, reasonable objections to imperativism that will remain and that are conclusive even at this level. For one thing, surely, moral judgments used to direct people's conduct cannot be used *merely* to direct their conduct: these cannot be merely imperatives, but must be imperatives thought to be *justified* on some grounds or other. And if this is so, then the judgment of what is morally appropriate or required, *on which the imperative logically depends for justification,* cannot itself be an imperative. Either so-called moral imperatives are arbitrary, without justification, or the admission of morally justified imperatives (directing conduct) presupposes a kind of moral judgment that is not itself an imperative. From this point of view, an imperatival function assigned to moral judgments can never be more than a subsidiary function. A second objection may trade on the important differences between first-, second-, and third-person discourse with respect to commands, orders, resolves, wishes, threats, advice, instruction, and the like. However similar second- and third-person discourse may be alleged to be (though even this is rather dubious in important cases and depends chiefly on grammatical ambiguities), first-person discourse is quite distinctively defective in relevant ways. I cannot command myself or give orders to myself or direct myself or threaten myself or advise myself or give instruction to myself; and though I can make my own resolutions, no one can make them for me. But moral judgments—in particular, 'ought'-judgments of the relevant sort—appear to be indifferent, in at least some respects bearing on conduct, to the distinctions of grammatical persons. And if this is so, then imperativism must be inadequate, for it would require that the sense of 'ought,' used in a morally relevant way, could not be univocal for first-, second-, and third-person discourse.

These arguments, however, leave the field open to alternative proposals. I wish to hold rather that, for example, moral judgments are simply not uniform, that no thesis like imperativism, no thesis of a universal property or use of moral judgments, will do. Concede, for the sake of the issue, that if imperativism obtains, it holds equally well for first-, second-, and third-person discourse. Now, consider a difficulty of another sort, that there are moral judgments that *cannot* defensibly be construed as action-guiding in any sense in which they may be supposed to *direct* conduct. H. A. Prichard, for example, correctly insisted that, however possible it might be that behaving in this or that way (open to deliberate choice) might lead us to become *courageous* or *loving*, acting courageously or with love (that is, acting from a certain motive), according to any account of human action, was not something one could deliberately do.[2] But, if that is the case, then the moral judgment that Peter acted with courage *cannot* be an action-guiding judgment; nor indeed can, if it is allowed, the judgment that one ought to act with courage. To hold that moral judgments are action-guiding, in the face of such counter-instances, is simply a mistake; contrariwise, to insist that such judgments are not moral judgments *because* they are not action-guiding is hardly helpful. This suggests two important themes, which we shall explore a bit further: for one thing, with reference to familiar disputes in moral philosophy, 'ought' need not imply 'can,' some 'ought'-judgments at least do not entail 'can'-judgments (and are, to that extent, not action-guiding); for another, judgments of character and motivation are, as such, not action-guiding judgments, though they be moral judgments.

It is normally inappropriate, we may observe, to say to someone that he ought to be a saint or ought to act in a saintly way. There are, of course, very many things that a man might deliberately do that would lead to his being brave or generous or just or the like; and, therefore, we may say that a man ought to be such or to behave in such a way under appropriate circumstances, even though a man cannot deliberately be such or deliberately behave in such a way. A saintly man might deliberately do what happens to be a saintly thing; but there are no formulable practices that remotely promise to produce a saint—too much depends on natural gifts of character. We can do no more than *appreciate* that a man is a saint (or a moral monster or the like): there is no relevant sense in which we could possibly *direct* anyone's conduct to accord with saintliness. Hare,[3] in such cases—as, for instance, in judging the life of St. Francis—denies that we are concerned with *moral* judgments or *moral* matters, *since* the judgments are clearly not action-guiding. But he might rather have admitted—what other sorts of cases confirm—that not all moral judgments, whether 'ought'-judgments or not, are action-guiding. We may, in making moral judgments, merely appreciate a man's character, in the sense of comprehending (independent of an analysis of the logical properties of the judgments involved) that a given judgment rightly fits a given man's character, or in the sense of savoring the qualities of his character so judged.

A moral judgment, then, may be directive (action-guiding); but, sometimes, it may be merely appreciative (and may actually not be able to be directive); and, sometimes, it may be merely informative, in the sense in which things are truly said to have a given property. There is absolutely no reason for insisting that all moral judgments, *qua* moral judgments, are, or must be, action-guiding. Some of them cannot be action-guiding; and of those that can, there is, in relevantly making the judgment itself, no logical constraint to direct anyone's life. For, as we have already seen, to direct another's conduct in a morally defensible way is tantamount to having made an antecedent moral judgment of a non-directive sort.

Any number of related considerations may be added. We say, for example, in certain circumstances, "There ought to be an end to war," "Men ought not to suffer unmerited misfortune," "All men ought to have an equal chance to be happy." Here, we attend to the presence of *evil* (surely, at least in part, morally relevant evil) that human efforts either cannot conceivably alter or cannot be expected to eliminate. We touch here on goals that relate to what men *are* able to effect; but the conditions in mind are ideal or perfect and, furthermore, no particular men are addressed or referred to in issuing a judgment of the relevant sort. These judgments are morally eligible without regard to the capacity of particular men and concern achievements that no men could conceivably effect, though the conditions in mind are conceivable and relate to human effort. The 'ought' of such judgments does not imply 'can' (in whatever sense is appropriate to directives) and the judgments themselves cannot be regarded as action-guiding in the required sense. Again, we advise a man, in certain circumstances, that "you ought to do what is right," "you ought to contribute to another's happiness," "you ought to be good." Here, we are not advising a man *to do* anything at all. Rather, we are pointing to the characteristic *reasons* for which morally motivated men act. Therefore, although such reasons do not apply unless men are able to act in particular ways, these reasons may be advanced and accepted without regard to any particular action whatsoever. Here, 'ought' does not imply 'can' and the corresponding judgments cannot be construed as action-guiding in the required sense. Again, we may say of a man, in certain circumstances, that "he ought to provide more adequately for his family," though we realize that, given his skills and opportunities, he cannot. We cannot be using the judgment in an action-guiding sense if we believe him to be incapable of the relevant action and if the judgment is pertinent *now*, pertinent to his present condition. But we may thereby draw attention to the fact that his family is entitled, has a moral right, to be taken better care of, quite independently of his capacity.

I think it is fair to say that, among all possible moral judgments, 'ought'-judgments are the ones that suggest the plausibility of the imperativist thesis. We have seen, however, that different sorts of such judgments need not, and even cannot, be construed as directive of conduct; in fact, it does not seem possible to assign to all the varieties of 'ought'-judgments one would acknowledge as morally relevant a single and uniform use like the directive use. Trivially, moral judgments are sentences used to judge. But there is no reason to suppose that the logical role we assign to sentences, in being used to make judgments, could possibly serve to distinguish not only moral judgments from aesthetic judgments or from medical judgments or from legal judgments, but also moral judgments (or any of the other sorts) from factual judgments. It seems impossible to deny that the only way of distinguishing one kind of judgment from another (as distinct from the uses to which they may be put) lies entirely with classifying the range of predicates that we employ. To speak of lying is to speak of a moral issue; to speak of a breach of contract is to speak of a legal issue; to speak of the balance of a painting, an aesthetic issue; and to speak of the malfunctioning of the kidney, a medical issue. Nevertheless, to offer paradigms is not to offer defining characteristics.

There are a number of distinctions I should like to collect at this point, that bear on the original issue of the non-uniformity of the uses and syntax of moral and aesthetic judgments and judgments of similar sorts. For one thing, the action-guiding or action-governing use of moral judgments—which is ordinarily emphasized as one of its most distinctive features—may be serviced in at least two quite different ways. In one, it may be serviced by the use of imperatives or by sentences that are used jointly to pass judgment and to direct conduct (as imperatives). And in a second, it may be serviced, in sentences used to judge (but not to direct) conduct, by a prominent sense of 'ought' proper to moral judgments. The first of these two alternatives, as we have already seen, requires that 'ought' not be univocal for first-, second-, and third-person discourse. But the second provides the needed univocity. We may say that to judge that one *ought* to do X (in the morally relevant sense) is to judge not only that the action involved is appropriate or right or obligatory according to some admitted rule or criterion, but also that anyone who would acknowledge that, in given circumstances, *he* ought to do X, would also intend to act in accord with what he recognizes he ought to do. That is, the force of 'ought' (relative to the judgment's action-guiding use) lies in its bearing on the conformity of conduct and judgment. If I judge that another ought to do X, under my breath, so to speak, I have not directed *him* to act in any way; but I should go on to judge his *conduct* as according or not according with what I judge he ought to do. And if I judge that *I* ought to do X, or concur with another that I ought to do X, then *grasping the sense of 'ought,'* I cannot *consistently* not intend to do X. I should christen this sort of consistency *consistency in practice,* or moral consistency, and I should admit further that one may be morally criticized for inconsistency of the relevant sort as well as for acting contrary to what one ought to do. If the account is accepted, then it is altogether possible to admit a variety of subsidiary linguistic acts, like persuading, ordering, resolving, threatening, advising, that may service moral ends and may, in so doing, employ the same term 'ought' in logically different ways. At the very least, the argument demonstrates that moral utterances may be assigned an action-guiding role without involving imperatives. But to admit that this role may be serviced both by imperatives and by the sense of 'ought' in moral utterances that are not imperatives is to admit, in an important regard, the non-uniformity of moral utterances themselves: they neither are, nor need to be, all imperatives.

A second point is this: moral utterances neither are, nor need to be, action-guiding. We have already pursued the matter in observing a variety of judgments that *cannot* be action-guiding in the required sense—judging that a man is a saint or moral monster, judging character and motivation, judging what is morally appropriate in circumstances in which we believe the agent involved to be incapable of fulfilling his responsibility. And we have already seen that, even with respect to judgments of what one ought to do, where these are action-guiding in some sense, the action-guiding role of moral utterances may be preserved without invoking imperatives; and construing imperatives as morally relevant is, in effect, presupposing judgments that merely identify what it is one ought to do. In short, there must, by any account, be a significantly large run of moral judgments that are *not* action-guiding, that we use in merely marking out what we notice or *appreciate* regarding what is right or good or obligatory or the like.

Now, I have previously argued that value judgments are not, *qua* judgments, all of the same logical sort, that we must admit, at the very least, the distinction between what I have called findings and appreciative judgments. I have tried to show further, in the present context, that moral judgments are not, and cannot, all be imperatives and are not, and cannot, all be action-guiding. But this means that moral judgments do not have a logically uniform use (as to direct conduct) or a logically uniform syntax (as being imperatives), nor are they confirmed in logically uniform ways (as being findings). There is, then, no possible way of distinguishing moral judgments from value judgments of other sorts, except perhaps by classifying exclusive sets of predicates; that is, there can be no comprehensive rule for the distinction, ranging over all value judgments, though this does not mean that particular judgments cannot reasonably be said to be moral *rather than* aesthetic judgments. *In context,* to judge that Peter murdered Mary may be to render a *legal* judgment. But it does not follow from deciding this that the judgment itself has *any* logically distinctive properties that could serve to mark it off as legal rather than as moral or aesthetic: the predicates alone or the use of sets of predicates in given contexts may decide the issue. To admit this, however, is to defeat a very persistent and widespread Kantian conviction.

The argument needs to be bolstered by considering non-moral

contexts. For one thing, whoever would cling to the Kantian view of value judgments (as distinct from Kant's own particular version of the view) would have to decide such questions as whether moral and legal judgments are to be assigned to significantly (relevantly) distinct domains of discourse, whether moral judgments and judgments of etiquette have overlapping or coextensive domains or whether etiquette is, as such, a moral concern or not. Not to be able to decide such issues—and their artificiality strikes us at once—is to cast doubt on the possibility of distinguishing sharply between the different kinds of value judgments by sorting out the ranges of relevant sets of predicates.

It is not difficult, for instance, to suppose that there are runs of predicates that may be taken to be jointly moral and aesthetic. Once I give up the prejudice that moral judgments are action-guiding and grant that they may register claims (of logically distinct sorts) that accord with what I notice or appreciate, it is no longer a simple matter to propose boundaries between the moral and the aesthetic. If I judge someone's conduct to be kindly or tactful or generous or discreet or gracious or foul, have I judged in a *morally* relevant (and therefore not aesthetically relevant) way or have I judged in an *aesthetically* (and therefore not morally) relevant way? There seems to be no ready answer, short of legislating boundaries *ad hoc*. In fact, *if* the thesis that judgments of the relevantly different sorts have markedly different logical properties itself falls, there remains hardly any point in insisting on a sharp demarcation among the different sorts of judgments themselves. That is, if judging that a man's conduct is gracious is (whatever the logical properties of such a judgment) a way of marking what I appreciate or notice respecting that man's conduct, what could I possibly be preserving in insisting that the judgment is moral *and* not aesthetic?

To say that the judgment registers what it is I appreciate or notice with respect to someone's conduct is *already* to identify an ulterior use (comparable to the directive use of moral judgments) for the sake of which alone I may issue the judgment;

and to identify that use—to provide for instance for what we might call *moral appreciation*—is to disorder the received (what I am calling the Kantian) view of the ulterior uses of distinctively moral and aesthetic judgments. Merely to have undermined the thesis of the directive use of moral judgments is to have seriously threatened the effort to sort out exclusive sets of predicates that may be assigned to the moral, the legal, the medical, the religious, the aesthetic, the prudential, the political, the economic domains; for, to have done so is to have eliminated the principal reason for arranging such a catalogue.

But not only may I employ predicates that are jointly moral and aesthetic (whether of the sort appropriate to findings or to appreciative judgments), I may also provide for the directive use (and other such uses) of value judgments in the aesthetic as well as in the moral domain. It is, in fact, a well-known thesis of Stuart Hampshire's,[4] that critical judgments of the aesthetic sort are non-committal, in the sense that they do not, and cannot, make recommendations about what an artist ought to do. One may prefer, or reject, a certain work of art without, Hampshire thinks, being required to propose what ought to have been done to improve it. It is true that one may not be *required* to propose an adjustment, but the same is true in the moral domain: I may see that what was done ought not to have been done without at all being able to suggest a better way of proceeding. Nevertheless, it may be appropriate and reasonably expected that a knowledgeable critic, in judging a work to be deficient, specify what indeed *ought to have been done* to improve the work. The only point to consider is that a directive, or action-guiding, judgment may properly be made in the aesthetic domain, which will behave in the same logical way as its counterpart in the moral domain. And if this is so, then we cannot segregate moral and aesthetic judgments either in terms of the uses to which these judgments may be put or in terms of the syntax of judgments of the two sorts. What would be the point of insisting that, for example, Ezra Pound's instruction to the young T. S. Eliot, that he ought to cut the length of *The Wasteland* and begin the poem with the line, "April is the cruellest month," was a moral or quasi-moral judgment and not an aesthetic judgment precisely because it *did* direct another's action? Judgments that express our appreciation may predominate in the aesthetic domain and judgments that direct conduct may predominate in the moral domain, but there are no convincing reasons for believing that non-directive judgments cannot occur in the moral domain or that directive judgments cannot occur in the aesthetic. And if this holds for what are traditionally radically different sorts of judgments, it is unlikely that any of the less clearly articulated domains of value judgments will lend themselves to a simple demarcation of the required sort.

The discussion of issues like emotivism and imperativism tends to obscure the range of characteristic uses to which value judgments may be put and the syntactical variety such judgments (and related utterances) may exhibit. Consider remarks made to commend something. Commending is very closely related to judging yet distinct from judging. In fact, the same sentences serve both functions. I may commend a man as a good barber and may judge him to be a good barber, saying in different contexts, "He's a good barber." Sometimes, we speak loosely of sentences used to commend as being value judgments, as, typically, when P. H. Nowell-Smith speaks of the fundamental use of 'good' to express a preference.[5] The critical distinction is this: commendations may call for explanation but not for justification; and judgments, of whatever sort they may be, call for justification. Judgments are open to error and may, depending on whether they are findings or appreciative judgments, be corrected and challenged in appropriate ways. The reasons for which someone commends something may provide grounds for rejecting someone's commendation; but a commendation is not the sort of thing that can be corrected. One may commend responsibly or irresponsibly, with or without *his* own reasons, conservatively, enthusiastically, arbitrarily; but one's judgment calls for support or defense. We think of a commendation primarily as an *action* of a certain sort, as the exhibition or expression of approval, preference, liking (as in answer to an inquiry or in conversation). And we think of a judgment primarily as a formulated *claim,* as a sentence whose truth or falsity or defensibility of other sorts may be assessed. But since the action of commending is, typically, verbal, the sentence deposited is readily construed as a judgment; and since we suppose an attitude or conviction, on the part of a speaker, congruent with his claims, we construe a value judgment as a commendation (or its reverse) as well. But to allow this conflating of distinctions is to acknowledge the complexity of our use of the relevant sentences, not the force of such theories as emotivism with respect to judgment proper.

Here lies the weakness, for example, of Nowell-Smith's thesis of the primacy of the commending use of 'good.' 'Good' used in its commending sense, as in "He's a good barber," has the sense merely of expressing approval and the like, independent of all considerations relevant to the defense of judgments, and therefore obliges us to construe the sentence uttered as a performative or quasi-performative of the same sort. By uttering the sentence, where 'good' is intended in its commending sense, I do commend. But 'good' used in a sense proper to judgment, as also in "He's a good barber," is never simply a one-place predicate. It is always an elliptical expression for any number of more complex predicates, such as 'good-in-such-and-such-a-respect,' 'good-as-of-such-a-kind.' We understand the predicate form 'good . . . ,' where the complexity of admissible entries is not indicated, to be occupied by valuational predicates; hence, we understand *judgments* like "He's very good," even though a context be lacking in which the ellipsis may be replaced by a fully explicit predicate. Furthermore, it is easy to see how, given the initial attraction of the imperativist thesis, one might be inclined to construe value judgments as commendations (and the like); but to do so is not merely to confuse judgments with what are not judgments, it is to fail to distinguish two quite distinct uses of 'good' and related expressions. In commendations, 'good' does not function as a predicate at all; and in judgments, it is an elliptical form for a variety of multi-placed predicates. G. E. Moore's mistake lay in assuming 'good' to designate a simple quality; Nowell-Smith's and Hare's, in confusing a non-predicative use of 'good' with its predicative use.

We may give our account a firmer sense of closure if we consider a further distinction. If commendations are sub-judgments, in calling not for defense or support but only for explanation—in that our commend*ing* is explained by reference to this or that reason—verdicts are super-judgments. *Qua* verdicts, valuational sentences foreclose on defense or support. Verdicts may be preceded or succeeded by value judgments; but if they are regarded as a kind of value judgment, once again a performative use of language will have been conflated with that use we are calling the making of a value judgment. Something is *assigned* a value by the mere issuing of a verdict. The value may have been responsibly assigned or it may not have been. Judicious appraisal may have preceded it, and it may, on review, be put aside on the strength of relevant *judgments*. But however we may suppose the judge or judges to have arrived at a verdict, a verdict does not, *qua* verdict, call for or require defense. Sentences may, of course, be used jointly for verdicts and judgments, just as they may, for commendations and judgments.

In beauty contests, for instance, and in many other contexts, "the opinion of the judges," as we say, "is final." We suppose the relevant information to have been antecedently supplied to the judges or to have been made available, and we suppose the judges to have sorted this out in accord with appropriate criteria. But characteristically, all we receive is a public verdict; and in many instances, we have not the faintest hint of the grounds on which it has been determined. *If* we construe the verdict *as* a judgment (as well we may), we may request supporting reasons. But verdicts (think of judging criminals, literary contests, dog shows) are typically rendered in contexts in which, though there may or may not be provision for appeals from a verdict, the judgment rendered is, *qua* verdict, decisive merely in having been issued appropriately. A defendant is guilty, in the context of verdicts, if he is judged guilty; the verdict may be appealed and a *higher* verdict may declare him innocent; or, we may supercede the context of verdicts altogether (as in reviewing court cases over coffee) and judge (even in the sense of a finding) that the defendant was innocent. 'Innocent' and 'guilty,' in verdicts, are predicates properly assigned merely by virtue of *rendering a verdict*; but 'innocent' and 'guilty' are also proper predicates for value judgments, and thus construed, their ascription is open to defense and a call for defense.

Also, generally speaking, verdicts are rendered in accord with antecedently designated distinctions: 'guilty,' 'innocent,' 'not proved'; 'First Prize,' 'Second Prize,' 'Third Prize'; 'best of breed,' 'best of show.' We do sometimes allow, in more informal settings, certain valuational remarks to pass for verdicts. For example, someone *whose judgment is particularly respected* judges your first efforts at poetry to be "fine" or "very promising" or the like. Here we see a possible convergence between commendations (or the reverse) and verdicts. Nevertheless, the difference remains clear: in a verdict, however formal or informal it may be, the value term is used predicatively—the difficulty being that there are no considerations bearing on the proper ascription of the predicate other than its having been ascribed by the assigned judge; and in a commendation, the value term is not being used predicatively at all but only to express or indicate a liking or preference or the like—with or without any indication that a counterpart judgment could be defended. A commendation is no judgment at all, and a verdict is, so to speak, a degenerate judgment; correspondingly, 'good' in the context of commendations is not a predicate, and 'good' in the context of verdicts is a degenerate predicate. The confusion of these two uses and the failure to distinguish either or both from the use of valuational predicates (proper in value judgments) is particularly marked in the accounts of Margaret Macdonald [6] and Arnold Isenberg;[7] and it was J. L. Austin's suspicion of both of these uses that led him to recommend a closer study of "the dumpy and the dainty." Isenberg treats verdicts and (what amount to) findings as expressions of preference or commendations, and Macdonald holds both that verdicts call for justification and that justification can only be of the sort accorded "our affections and antipathies," our tastes (or what amounts to appreciative judgments).

Value judgments themselves, of course, exhibit further variety. We distinguish appraisals, gradings, rankings, assessments, as well as a great many other sorts of judgments not sufficiently formalized to be distinctively labeled. Judgments of these sorts may be either findings or appreciative judgments; and they may also have verdict-like aspects. The appraisal of a jeweler, for example, may combine, in judging a diamond, considerations of weight and purity (relevant to findings), considerations of the beauty of the cutting (relevant to appreciative judgments and/ or findings), and considerations of price, as in an offer of purchase (relevant to verdicts). But however interesting these varieties and complex forms may be, the principal distinction rests with contrasting value judgments proper with the related uses of valuationally significant sentences with which they may be confused; and, correspondingly, with contrasting the fully predicative use of value terms, in value judgments, and the non-predicative, or degenerately predicative, use of value terms in commendations and verdicts. Furthermore, returning to our opening remarks, there are no reasons for supposing that any of these distinctions regarding valuational sentences and valuational terms are linked in any logically important or exclusive way with the distinctions usually made between the various kinds of value judgments—as being moral or aesthetic or legal or prudential or the like.

There remains, nevertheless, an important difference between moral judgments and (with a crucial *caveat*) value judgments of every other sort—a difference already noted at the very beginning of this account; for, moral considerations are, as such, occupied with whatever are thought to be the overriding values of human life. As far as the foregoing argument is concerned, this feature of moral judgments is irrelevant, for it does not of itself affect the question of the uses or the syntax of such judgments; and, as we have already seen, it could not serve to segregate the logical features of moral judgments as opposed to judgments of other sorts. Its importance lies, rather, with the provision of a much larger frame of reference than that of merely semantical or syntactical or pragmatic distinctions.

It might be thought that there are substantial pragmatic differences between moral judgments and value judgments of other sorts—where action-guiding considerations are relevant. But, although this is an understandable assumption, it cannot be supported. In the context, for instance, in which a thief is committed to attempting a robbery, it is quite clear that, if he believes that a certain strategy is the best one to follow under the circumstances, it would be inconsistent on his part—in a sense already supplied, in the sense of an appropriate, a rational, conformity between belief and practice—not to intend to act in accord with that strategy. It is irrelevant here that the end-in-view can hardly be construed, as such, as occupied with overriding values. The pragmatic question of the relationship between belief and conduct remains entirely unchanged whether one is facing a merely technical decision, *given* one's shifting interests and goals, or whether one is facing what a rational man (as I have argued) cannot avoid facing, namely, a moral scrutiny of his conduct, a scrutiny in terms of his putatively overriding values. There is a difference to be marked out—an important difference—but it is not concerned narrowly with the pragmatic aspects of the value judgments one actually *makes;* it concerns rather the implications of actually *making* value judgments. Let me explain.

The critical difference, as far as rationality is concerned, be-

tween moral and non-moral issues bearing on conduct, is simply
that a rational agent cannot fail, in a way that governs his review
of all of his behavior—actual or contemplated—to be attentive
to the congruity between particular projects, choices, decisions,
and the like and the overriding values to which he subscribes;
whereas, from this very point of view, no other goals, values,
projects, or the like are binding on him (unless conditionally, on
his actual interests, tastes, convictions, and commitment). *If* a
man chooses to be a thief, then, rationally, he will seek whatever means best serves his end conformably with other particular
ends to which he is also committed; but if he does not choose
to be a thief, then there are no rational constraints on him to
coordinate his behavior with any of the relevant goals of a thief.
If the argument holds for such technical goals (following Kant),
it will hold for all particular kinds of goals that we may label
medical, legal, economic, prudential, aesthetic, and the like.
But a moral concern, given the categorical sense of 'moral' already introduced, cannot be avoided by a rational agent: if he
has any personal interests at all, which he rationally pursues,
then (again in a somewhat Kantian spirit) he cannot fail to
consider the bearing of these enterprises on his beliefs about the
overriding values of life.[8] In fact, this thesis comes rather close,
I believe, to the point of Kant's formulating the concept of the
Categorical Imperative, without at all committing us to the substance of his own ethical theories.

The upshot is that, as one cannot rationally avoid moral reflection but may have quite idiosyncratic, contingent interests, one
is obliged to face the problem of cognitive claims respecting
overriding values. This problem *may* also arise for values of
other sorts; for example, one may claim to discover "true" aesthetic or medical or legal values or the like—and influential theorists have, from time to time, done so—though it is quite possible
to construe such values merely in terms of conventional, professional, institutionalized, or quite personal interests, without
pretending that the governing values are in any cognitively

relevant sense *discovered*. But, although this is, arguably, possible for non-moral values as well, the cognitive issue has, understandably, been most seriously pursued in the moral context, precisely because one is rationally enjoined to assess all of one's behavior in terms of the overriding values to which one is committed. If one must, rationally, do so, then—so the argument might go—it is important to know whether there are normative, overriding values open, in any sense at all, to discovery. If there are, the rational agent will of course be governed by these; and if there are not, he will be obliged to consider the coherence of his moral concern and actual conduct under this condition. Obviously, therefore, the claims of cognitivism play an altogether focal role in the formulation of an adequate moral philosophy.

We may look at the issue in another way. Normative values are values that, in context, take precedence over other putative values of a relevant sort. For instance, if we may speak of what is normatively beautiful, then at least in the ordering or ranking of things that have some justifiable claim to beauty, whatever is normatively beautiful will rank highest in the series; what follows pragmatically, it may be observed, is quite debatable (certainly nothing regarding pleasure or enjoyment or interest or even regarding the need to alter one's orientation or one's efforts at instruction). Overriding values, on the other hand, are normative values that take precedence over all other values as far as the conduct of one's life is concerned; they are, therefore, contextless, in the sense that a rational agent is essentially and—as one might say—globally concerned with the conduct of his life. *If* normative values were, in some fair sense, discoverable, then *if* they also had the relevant interests (aesthetic, medical, legal, and the like), human agents would, rationally, be bound to adjust their behavior to realize such values in their relevant projects. And if normative moral values were discoverable, then *since* such values are also overriding values and hence rational agents must be assumed to have the relevant interests, human agents would be bound to adjust their behavior to realize such values through their entire lives. Here, the junction of the claims of cognitivism and the distinction of moral questions would (if the former were vindicated) exhibit its most characteristic force. It is easy to see, for instance, that, given the nature of the moral concern and admitting the tenability of particular cognitive claims regarding the overriding values of life, men may judge and criticize and even *blame* and *condemn* one another for actions committed, without at all consulting *whether* the agent involved actually subscribed to moral ends, in any sense resembling that in which, say, he was clearly and personally interested in preserving his physical health. The unconditional (or, as Kant would put it, the categorical) force of moral judgments in general depends on the nature of the moral concern itself, but the force of particular judgments on the conduct of particular men depends on the tenability of cognitivism with respect to the relevant values. Without this combination, the very nature of moral criticism and condemnation as well as of the pragmatic consistency between belief and conduct are placed in at least apparent jeopardy, for it then becomes difficult to see how a rational moral agent can, in judging others, be anything but a partisan favoring his own preferred values or, in committing himself to the overriding values he adopts, succeed in distinguishing his moral from his merely contingent and passing interests (in particular, his prudential interests). But to say this is merely to identify once again the biographically affecting quality of the cognitivist claim.

CHAPTER 3

The Analysis of 'Ought' (I)

THE USE OF 'OUGHT' in moral judgments is the stumbling-block of metaethical theories. For one thing, its being, grammatically, an auxiliary verb raises serious questions about the systematic relations that hold between it and words like 'good' and 'right,' that, as adjectives, appear to occupy an attributive or predicative position. It poses, clearly, a challenge to our theory about value judgments, inasmuch as the distinction of 'ought'-judgments depends on the nature of its copula rather than on a range of predicates. Also, the notorious question whether 'ought' can be derived from 'is' presupposes that the critical distinction between value judgments and factual judgments depends on the verbs employed rather than on predicative expressions. For another thing, since 'ought'-judgments are taken to be paradigms of moral judgments and since, as moral judgments, they are prominently used in an action-guiding way, it appears dubious that moral judgments (and, in particular 'ought'-judgments) can be satisfactorily construed as statements of an indicative sort. The suggestion has been pursued, for example, that 'ought' is a modal operator of some kind; and another notorious question, whether " 'ought' implies 'can,' " has been made to depend on the allegedly action-guiding function of moral 'ought'-judgments. I have already broached these issues—and, in fact, suggested the lines of some solutions—but, in fairness to the importance of the implied challenge, I shall analyze 'ought' directly.

There are some preliminary considerations that may be mentioned, that promise both an economy in argument and an increase in its effectiveness. First of all, one should, if possible, hold to a univocal sense of 'ought,' regardless of the variety of contexts in which 'ought'-sentences occur. If, for instance, it could be argued that 'ought' is used in substantially the same sense in the following sentences,

1) He ought to be home in about twenty minutes
   (meaning that he may be expected to arrive
   there in about twenty minutes),

2) He ought to be earning a better salary
   (meaning that his capacities are greater
   than his financial returns),

3) He ought to take his son to a psychiatrist
   (meaning that the child is exhibiting some
   disorder),

4) He ought to return the money
   (meaning that he has stolen it),

a considerable gain in simplicity would be effected: the burden of proof would normally rest, surely, with whoever would claim a given expression is used in multivocal senses when a univocal sense is assignable and adequate. Now, certain restricted, well-known interpretations of 'ought'-sentences are open to objection on related grounds: the imperativist theory of moral 'ought'-sentences, thus, requires either that we provide first-person and past-tense imperatives—which is anomalous, or that we construe first-person and past-tense sentences as logically subsidiary locutions depending on "primary" second-person moral utterances—which is purely *ad hoc* and unnecessary.[1]

A second consideration is this: it seems reasonable to distinguish the sense and criteria of use of 'ought,' rather along the same lines as is generally conceded for the term 'good.' Clearly, we understand the meaning of 'good' in its characteristic use, though we may not know by what criteria anything in question is being relevantly judged to be good. It is fair to hold that 'good' is univocal, in speaking of a good man, a good dog, a good thief, a good specimen; but it may not be at all clear, in grasping the meaning of what is said, what criteria of goodness are being called into play. An analogous distinction, I should maintain, may be applied to the use of 'ought': in the four specimen sentences offered above, it may thus be held (we must consider this possibility) that 'ought' is univocal. Yet it may also be admitted that the reasons for asserting what corresponds to the content of our four specimens are, surely, of strikingly different sorts; consequently, it seems reasonable as well to hold that, in different contexts, we appeal to different criteria in terms of which to judge that something *ought* to be the case or to obtain or to be done. We may put the point a little more lucidly: if one is to attempt to assign, with any possibility of success, a univocal sense to 'ought,' it will be necessary to distinguish between its sense and criteria of use—but, given familiar analyses of 'good,' there is a relevant precedent for doing so.[2]

Those, however, who wish to construe 'ought' as a deontic operator of some sort stress either or both of two distinct sorts of considerations. For one, they attempt to support a strong analogy between the putative deontic operators, 'obligatory,' 'permissible,' and 'forbidden,' and the alethic operators 'necessary,' 'possible,' and 'impossible.'[3] But, of course, if 'ought' has a univocal sense for sentences of the sorts already provided, the deontic force of 'ought,' in the restricted context of use in certain sentences only, will have to be assigned to aspects of the use of 'ought' other than its sense—perhaps to the criteria of its use or to properties of sentences or to ulterior, pragmatic uses of sentences. The attempt to develop a deontic analysis of the sense of 'ought' presupposes plural senses of 'ought' for such a range of sentences as we have sampled, since the first three of our four samples cannot be construed deontically. Another way of putting the same point, which is instructive, is that 'ought' and 'obligatory' are not synonymous or equivalent expressions and that, even in the moral setting, 'ought'-judgments need not concern what is obligatory or what one is obliged to do. But if the doctrine that 'ought' implies 'can' is false, even when confined to the moral setting (it is obviously false, ranging over sentences like our specimens), then the hoped-for parallelism between the deontic and alethic operators must be defective (since 'can' is the only plausible analogue of 'possible'). Of course, the parallelism is defective in other respects, since what is necessary is actual and what is actual is possible; but there is no corresponding relationship for the deontic operators: even what is obligatory need not be actual and what is actual may well be forbidden. One is also tempted to say that what is obligatory ought to be, or ought to be done, which suggests (rightly, I think) that 'obligatory' does not provide the sense or part of the sense of 'ought' but is itself to be explicated in terms of 'ought.' Certainly, it may be said that a good swimmer *ought* to try to save the life of a drowning man if he can, but it is excessive, if he is merely a bystander, to claim that he is *obliged* to do so, or that it is *obligatory* for him to do so. In any event, without a clarification of the sense of 'ought,' it is quite unconvincing to construct modal parallels between alethic and deontic operators. For, if 'ought'-judgments governing actions do not require or presuppose an agent's capacity to act in the way judged, in the relevant circumstances (which is, as I say, contrary to the only promising basis for the parallels alleged), the entire program is threatened. The modal interpretation characteristically presupposes the doctrine of "'ought' implies 'can,'" but that doctrine is certainly debatable (even in the moral context)—I should myself say, quite false. Semantic considerations, therefore, that support the univocity of 'ought' definitely go against a deontic analysis of the sense of the *moral* 'ought'; alternatively put, an axiomatized deontic system remains in need of an admissible interpretation—regardless of its formal elegance.

It must be admitted, however, that there are *some prima facie* parallels between the would-be deontic operators, 'obligatory,' 'permissible,' and 'forbidden' and the alethic operators, 'necessary,' 'possible,' and 'impossible'; but these parallels may well be preserved without insisting on the syntactical thesis regarding operators (particularly as the notion of an "operator" is itself quite obscure syntactically—if we seek a uniform description suitable to the so-called alethic, epistemic, and deontic operators). The apparent parallel is simply the opening wedge for the argument but by itself is by no means conclusive. To emphasize, as we have, the untenability of the doctrine that 'ought' implies 'can,' the untenability of imperativism, the univocity of 'ought' for ranges to include, but not to be restricted to, the range of moral judgments, the implausibility of construing 'ought' deontically for ranges of non-moral judgments, and the non-equivalence of 'ought' and 'obligatory' even within the moral domain, is to muster relatively powerful counter-arguments against both the modal thesis and the deontic-operator thesis.

The second sort of consideration favoring the view that 'ought' is a deontic operator of some sort is that it can be added to relatively simple sentences in order to form sentences of additional complexity—whether the connection be truth- or non-truth-functionally construed. It is well-known, however, that, although plausible grammatical adjustments will allow the thesis to be applied to particular actions by way of being applied to singular statements concerning particular actions, it does not appear to lend itself with any success to 'ought'-judgments concerning types of actions.[4] Nevertheless, there is no *prima facie* reason for supposing that 'ought' is not being used univocally in judgments about particular actions and in judgments about types of actions. Furthermore, even with respect to particular actions, deontic theorists are inclined to invent strenuous interpretations of 'ought'-judgments, in order to provide for a distinctive operator—for instance, that if the state of affairs specified by the constituent sentence not obtain, sanctions will be applied (which, apart from the dubious accuracy of the paraphrase, is self-trivializing by an acknowledgment that either the sanctions will be applied or they *ought* to be); or, again, that the deontic operator converts an imperative into an indicative—which compounds the difficulties of the imperativist with those of construing sentences that do not appear to be imperatives as imperatives (and which is further complicated by the obvious fact that 'ought'-judgments may be formulated "in one's heart" and, therefore, outside of a context of commanding or directing another).

The general problem confronting theorists who wish to construe 'ought' as a deontic operator is, quite simply, that their ingenuity is exercised to the limit in interpreting familiar sentences in accord with their thesis. Under these circumstances, it is less relevant to insist on the truth or falsity of the thesis than it is to compare the complexity and possible arbitrariness of its assumptions and application with the corresponding features of alternative models. It seems eminently reasonable, in this regard, that the logically simpler and more comprehensive model be preferred, if there are no antecedently decisive reasons for insisting that any eligible model incorporate particular features that are somehow given—for instance, that 'ought' be taken to be a separable operator that may be added to sentences to form more complex sentences—and where the features selected themselves generate puzzles of at least comparable complexity.

The simpler thesis I propose undercuts both sorts of considerations mentioned, that might favor the construing of 'ought' as a deontic operator. I claim that 'ought'-sentences of the familiar sort, including such specimen sentences as have been provided above, are all in the indicative mood, capable of being true and false, and not, solely for the reason that 'ought' is the principal verb, a complex sentence formed by adding an operator to a simpler, independent sentence. Furthermore, 'ought,' for the entire range of sentences suggested by our specimens, is univocal on the thesis proposed. I cannot see, if the thesis can be shown to fit such sentences, that there would be the slightest reason to prefer the alternatives already broached. Let us, therefore, consider the thesis in some detail.

Respecting its sense, I suggest that 'ought' has the force of a predicate expression rather than of a verb or auxiliary verb: in suitable transformations for example, it might well have appeared as 'oughtful.'[5] It is used to characterize some item as superior or first in rank or preference or the like among a set of relevant alternatives, in some respect to be supplied in context; the respect in which such ordering obtains governs the relevant criteria of appraisal. Thus, for instance, our first specimen sentence, "He ought to be home in about twenty minutes," may be paraphrased roughly (and somewhat explicitly) as, "That he will be home in about twenty minutes is the likeliest estimate of his location in about twenty minutes." Our second specimen, "He ought to be earning a better salary" may be similarly paraphrased, "A better salary is more commensurate with his standing than his present salary." Our third specimen, "He ought to take his son to a psychiatrist" may be paraphrased, "To take his son to a psychiatrist would be the most helpful way of handling his condition." And our fourth specimen, "He ought to return the money" may be paraphrased, "Returning the money is the most appropriate thing to do under the circumstances." I have deliberately made the paraphrases relatively vague as far as the substantive issues are concerned, in order to stress the respect in which we may distinguish the sense of 'ought' from the criteria of its use (and, even more seriously, from the justification of the claim in question). There are important benefits, as we shall see, that follow. But, for the moment, I wish to emphasize that, allowing for the enormous difficulty of translation and of fixing synonymy, it has been possible to assign a univocal sense to 'ought' that does not appear to do violence to the sense of a range of extremely varied sentences. I find it unlikely that similar paraphrases could not be supplied for the entire stock of relevant sentences. Of course, all of our specimens may be converted into questions: we see, therefore, that the univocity of 'ought' can survive a change in grammatical mood. And should one concede—as is sometimes suggested—

that the thesis that 'ought' is an operator can be converted to a thesis about predicate expressions, the apparent quarrel (but also the evident mystery) may be summarily shelved.

If we construe judgments that might employ our specimen sentences in suitable contexts, we can specify relevant criteria by which to appraise whether indeed what is claimed actually is the case. From this point of view, if there are assignable criteria by which to judge the claims, the claims in question are straightforwardly factual. The original motivation for an imperativist reading of 'ought'-judgments was an interest in accommodating, without adopting intuitionism, G. E. Moore's exposure of the Naturalistic Fallacy. But that issue may be entirely neutralized, in our present setting, once it is seen—as has already been shown—that the question between naturalistic and non-naturalistic views of goodness and rightness and the like, concerns, exclusively, the ascription of predicates and not the truth value of sentences and assertions.

Now, then, there are no restrictions that can be imposed on the variety of criteria (and underlying purposes) with respect to which 'ought'-judgments may be made, except that the criteria must be such as to allow us to rank members of a set of relevant alternatives in terms of some designated feature. Thus, in our first specimen, clearly, the context is a predictive one: alternative predictions are to be ranked in terms of likelihood or plausibility or the like, with regard to some information that is available. In our second specimen, the context is one of the commensurability or fitness between talents or status or skill or the like and an assigned salary taken as a gauge of official recognition of talents or status or skill or the like. In our third specimen, the context is one of action and decision relative to the promotion of health, that is, given that health is the governing concern. And in our fourth specimen, the context is one of moral concern, in which we are to consider what is the right or best thing to do or the like, in the circumstances given. By this simple enumeration, we see the substantial simplification of the analysis of 'ought' that is worked merely by distinguishing the sense and criteria of use of 'ought,' construed as a predicate.

Once the distinction is allowed, we shall find it relatively easy to account for a number of well-known features of 'ought'-judgments, particularly the feature of being action-guiding. Here, probably, the most useful detail to notice concerns the different functions of the verbal expressions, 'ought to be' and 'ought to do' or 'ought to be done' or their cognates. Thus, the sense of 'ought' must be supplemented by the criteria of its use; and the selection of relevant criteria raises, in varying ways, questions of consistency between belief and action (or expectation). Our first and second specimens employ the first of these expressions; they are not, in context, action-guiding, but they could be. *If* anyone's conduct and deliberate behavior were relevantly affected by the movements of the person in question, in the first specimen, then to be guided by the best prediction about such movements that one can obtain under the circumstances is to act rationally. Similarly, if one were able and concerned to reward in a relevant financial way the merit or standing of employees, then, in our second specimen, he would be behaving rationally if, believing that a discrepancy obtained, he would, to that extent, be inclined to increase the salary of the person in question. As our specimen sentences stand, they are not linked to action-guiding considerations; they correspond merely to beliefs about certain states of affairs. But it does appear as if all 'ought'-judgments are focused on human expectations and at least possible actions: the whole idea of ranking alternatives suggests this. And, in general, the action-guiding function of 'ought'-judgments (and any other relevant judgments) is called into play only on the assumption that some agent in question is suitably motivated, so that entailed beliefs bear, rationally, on prospective actions.

Our third and fourth specimens, employing, as they do, cognates of 'ought to do,' are directly connected with action-guiding considerations; they correspond, in fact, with what, in Kantian terms, may be called hypothetical and categorical judgments. Again, they may be linked with the notion of rational conduct: thus, with respect to the third specimen, that, given the goal of promoting health, one would, rationally, choose the most helpful means to further health; and with respect to the fourth, that acting in a morally appropriate way is, *ipso facto*, acting rationally, since moral considerations are overriding considerations. In a word, 'ought'-judgments, in so far as they are accepted or believed by a human agent, raise, in given contexts, questions about consistency between belief and action.

The most strenuous form of this question arises in the moral context, which provides the paradigm of action-guiding judgments. For, as we say, a man ought actually to do what we judge rightly he ought to do. Nevertheless, if what has been previously claimed (though not conclusively defended) is true—that the thesis that 'ought' implies 'can' is untenable even in the moral domain—then it is altogether possible that a man believe that he ought to act in such and such a way and yet, in the relevant circumstances, fail to act not merely through reasons of ignorance, inadvertence, change of heart, or the like but also (a decisive possibility) because of an incapacity to act. The consistency or congruence between belief and action that we are concerned with here must accommodate such a possibility. We may say, then, that a man is morally consistent if, believing he can act relevantly, he intends to act thus; and, believing he cannot, he would intend to act thus if he could. But it is most certainly the case that a man may, in a morally relevant sense, believe that he ought to act in a certain specified way at the same time that he is inclined to act, or actually does act, against his belief. This, contrary to Hare's view,[6] tells not against his belief but against his consistency. Belief and action are, in the relevant respect, only contingently connected.

We see, therefore, the complexity of the action-guiding function of moral 'ought'-judgments: an agent must accept the truth of a judgment that *he* ought to act in such-and-such a way, in order to be relevantly guided; believing that moral judgments are true entails accepting the categorical force of such judgments; a man's moral consistency concerns his intention to act in accord with his judgment, conditional on his belief that he can so act. One of the by-benefits of this proposal is that it makes altogether unnecessary the (independently dubious) first-person commands and imperatives required by the imperativist. For, the admitted action-guiding function of moral judgments can thereby be accommodated without any commitment to a controversial theory of the grammar of moral sentences. Corresponding forms of consistency or congruence between belief and action are, clearly, analogous to moral consistency, except that the particular purposes or goals of the agent must be supplied.

Very likely, however, the most powerful benefit of our thesis lies in its bearing on the much-worked issue of deducing 'ought' from 'is.' The perplexities that have been generated since Hume's day may, quite plausibly, be attributed to an implicit acceptance of Hume's own way of insisting on the crucial replacement of the *verb* 'is' by the *verb* 'ought.' [7] Informal arguments seem quite convincing, of course, in spite of this. For example, the following appear to be valid arguments:

> Murder is morally condemned.
> If Peter takes Paul's life, Peter will murder Paul.
> Therefore, Peter ought not to take Paul's life.

> Peter is committed to promoting his health.
> Peter has tuberculosis and tuberculosis threatens health unless treated.

> Therefore, Peter ought to have his tuberculosis treated.

There are a number of things to be noted here. For one thing, it is easy to make such arguments appear puzzling by construing the conclusions as non-indicative, possibly imperative.[8] But we have already seen how the action-guiding function of 'ought'-judgments may be accommodated without adopting such a view. Secondly, such arguments construed as exhibiting straightforwardly syllogistic or similar forms may be said not to capture the essential features of the so-called practical syllogism explored by Aristotle.[9] But it is one of the economies of our account that questions of *rationality* (as involving no more than consistency between belief and action, given this or that motivation) simply do not require the assumption of a distinct (and independently puzzling) formal or quasi-formal mode of argument: one's conduct may be judged by reference to criteria of consistency without construing it (or some surrogate) somehow as the conclusion of a syllogism. Thirdly, the first premisses, respectively, of our two informal arguments may be interpreted as crypto-'ought'-judgments of some sort. But that Peter is concerned to promote his health appears to be a straightforward matter of fact regarding some of his purposes and objectives: given that he is thus committed, the 'ought'-judgment follows. It is somewhat more difficult to resist construing the first premiss of the moral argument as a crypto-'ought'-judgment, but we can, if we see that the first premiss supplies the *reason* for the 'ought'-judgment itself—what are taken to be the overriding values—and if we see that the criteria for appraising Peter's action, in context, presupposes a belief in a set of moral values. The difficulty here has more to do really with constructing an informal syllogism than with interpreting the premiss. This may be seen, perhaps, in arguments that relate to what may be termed "duties of office," statements of which are clearly in the indicative mood (though the question of the truth of such statements may be left unsettled here), for instance, the argument:

> Physicians have a duty to treat their patients so as to promote their health.
> Peter is Paul's physician.
> Therefore, Peter ought to treat Paul so as to promote his health.

A crucial part of the thesis is that there is no sharp demarcation line between factual judgments and value judgments.

But I have already suggested how to defend this view, namely, by distinguishing between the truth value of statements and the valuational or non-valuational nature of predicates. It is a fact that, in a moral or professional context, physicians are taken to have certain duties. Now then, whether or not having a duty is construed as equivalent to its being the case that one ought to act in a certain way, 'ought'-statements will be deducible from 'is'-statements. That murder is morally condemned is a fact respecting the moral domain, and this is so whether or not 'morally condemned' is construed as roughly equivalent to 'ought not.' (Questions about moral cognition may, of course, be ignored here.) The upshot is interesting. For, if the morally relevant premiss is construed as an 'ought'-statement of some sort, the admission will not affect the deduction of an 'ought' from an 'is,' since—according to our view—'ought' functions as a predicate expression that may be used in sentences in the indicative mood; and if the *moral* premiss may be a factual statement that is not an 'ought'-statement, then, of course, it is doubly clear that, in *non-moral* contexts, arguments are easily constructed in which (with premisses positing particular interests) 'ought'-statements may be derived from 'is'-statements that are *not* themselves 'ought'-statements.

Even so, I believe that the specimen moral arguments provided (and endless others as well) may plausibly be construed as depending on moral premises that are not 'ought'-statements. The defense of this view is relatively straightforward. For, moral values are overriding values, values that, by definition, take precedence over all other values as far as conduct is concerned: relevant premises, then, serve to affirm particular moral values. Conclusions, on the other hand, that take the form of 'ought'-judgments, serve to assert that to act in a certain way either accords or does not accord (in terms of consistency of belief and practice) with such values; hence, it is entirely appropriate to conclude that one *ought* to act in a morally suitable way, that is, that acting thus conforms with preferential moral ranking.

The categorical force of moral 'ought'-judgments corresponds to the overriding force of moral values relative to others, though questions may arise about the admissibility of particular values. Other (non-moral) 'ought'-judgments concerning values lack such force, since, precisely, whatever force they have is relative to the given interests and purposes of particular agents. For this reason, it is understandable that one might wish to construe premisses like "Murder is morally condemned" as crypto-'ought'-judgments, since they implicitly convey the sense of moral ranking. But it is not at all necessary to view them thus, for the logical force of the argument, as far as the *conclusion* is concerned, is precisely the same as that of arguments of the relevant non-moral variety; the ulterior question of the categorical nature of moral preference is a distinctly separate issue. The force of moral arguments respecting *conduct* bears, so to speak, on the question of *consistency* that has previously been raised; but the merely logical force of such arguments does not appear to be at all different from that in which a non-moral use of 'ought' is involved. The one question concerns the relationship between argument (or conclusion) and conduct; the other, the internal properties of the arguments themselves.

The sense of 'ought,' then, it may be claimed, remains univocal, though the criteria of its use vary and though distinctive questions of consistency of belief and action arise with the different criteria of use. For instance, if I say to someone at the dinner table, who is having trouble cutting his steak with his butter knife: "You ought to use your steak knife," it is altogether possible that he agree with the judgment and yet continue to use his butter knife—that is, without necessarily being inconsistent in the relevant sense. For, in agreeing, he may merely be acknowledging that the steak knife is more efficient than the butter knife for cutting steak, even though he has other reasons for persisting in using the butter knife (for instance, he wishes nastily to convey to the other guests how tough and difficult to cut the steak is). Routinized life makes the appeal to criteria of efficiency and etiquette quite appropriate in judging what one ought to do with regard to making eating effective and polite; but in itself this cannot guarantee what motives or interests particular eaters may have, and *this* bears on judgments of consistency between belief and action. This is a particularly sensitive issue in the moral context. For, if I were to agree that someone ought to help that man who is sinking in quicksand before our eyes, it is not in the least clear that I should be inconsistent if I thereupon failed to make an effort to help him. For one thing, I might merely watch with interest the rescue operations that others are engaged in; and for another, not supposing myself under any obligation to act, I might merely watch with some sadness as the man slowly disappears in the sand. I may very well be open to moral criticism as inconsiderate or unfeeling or lacking in courage or the like but not, for such reasons, open to the criticism of moral inconsistency. What the correct gauge of consistency is, both in moral and non-moral contexts, is extremely difficult to fix, as the question arises in remarkably refined and detailed ways. But to notice the problem is to see at once the important implications of distinguishing carefully between 'ought' and 'obligatory' and between the usual moral judgments and judgments of moral consistency.

Our relatively simple thesis respecting the analysis of 'ought,' therefore, seems to be compatible with, and is indeed particularly well-suited to, the strongest views on the chief issues—the constancy of the meaning of 'ought' across distinct contexts of use and the variability of relevant criteria of appraisal, the action-guiding feature of 'ought'-judgments and the use of 'ought' in judgments that are not action-guiding, the question of consistency between belief and action respecting the acceptance of 'ought'-judgments, the logical properties of the practical syllogism, the bearing of the falsity of the doctrine that 'ought' implies 'can,' the solution of the problem of deducing 'ought' from 'is,' the replacement of imperativism, accommodation of the charge of the Naturalistic Fallacy, connections between 'ought' and other value predicates (for, according to our view, relevant ranking of alternatives must be made in terms of alleged goodness, rightness, and the like), and finally, the possibility of avoiding modal and deontic-operator interpretations of 'ought.' I cannot see that there are any other issues of comparable importance that any theory respecting the analysis of 'ought' would be expected to face. And I cannot see that there is any alternative theory that fits defensible views on all of these issues as well.

CHAPTER 4

The Analysis of 'Ought' (II)

PRESCRIPTIVISM is a most strategically placed metaethical theory, for its tenability bears directly on the two best-known doctrines involving the moral use of 'ought': the doctrine " 'ought' implies 'can' " and the doctrine " 'ought' cannot be derived from 'is.' " The truth of prescriptivism entails the truth of " 'ought' implies 'can' " and the falsity of the latter entails the falsity of the former. Also, the truth of prescriptivism entails the truth of " 'ought' cannot be derived from is' " and the falsity of the latter entails the falsity of the former. We have already considered assorted reasons for thinking that prescriptivism is false, that the doctrine " 'ought' implies 'can' " is false, and that " 'ought' cannot be derived from 'is' " is false. *Descriptivism,* we may say (adjusting a term used in a variety of ways), is the thesis that value judgments (and, in particular, moral judgments) include findings, that is, judgments that are in the indicative mood and that can be confirmed as true or false. (Descriptivism, from this point of view, is not to be identified with cognitivism: both because it is logically possible to be a cognitivist and a prescriptivist [as in holding the Lord's Commandments to be revealed] and because the cognitive issues, as has already been acknowledged, remain entirely undecided in determining the logical properties of value judgments.) But the truth of descriptivism entails the falsity of " 'ought' cannot be derived from 'is,' " since 'ought'-judgments are themselves to be construed descriptively, if the descriptivist thesis is to be taken in any comprehensive way at all; restricted to non-'ought'-judgments, the thesis might still be true but substantially less interesting. Also, the descriptivist thesis is entirely neutral to that of " 'ought' implies 'can,' " in contrast with prescriptivism. There is, therefore, a very interesting nest of issues that systematically depend on the analysis of 'ought.'

The truth is that our previous objections to prescriptivism were largely directed to imperativism although not exclusively, since we did consider objections to the thesis that moral judgments are essentially action-guiding. If, of course, prescriptivist judgments are essentially action-guiding, then if action-guiding judgments presuppose that 'ought' implies 'can,' then if the latter doctrine is false, prescriptivism is false as well. So let us try to strengthen our position by demonstrating that the dictum " 'ought' implies 'can' " is false for the most central range of cases conceivable. R. M. Hare, it may be noted, a prominent prescriptivist, is persuaded that there are no satisfactory counter-instances, though he concedes the decisiveness of the issue.[1]

In advancing the argument, however, I am content to admit the most generous sense to 'implies' in the dictum: that, say, the sense of implication is not that of logical entailment but involves a weaker relationship of some sort.[2] And I am content to allow a generous reading of 'can' in the dictum, so that even 'believes that one can' may be substituted in appropriate instances. I am content also to allow the strongest sense to 'ought,' so that if one believes that he ought to act in a certain way (in a morally relevant context) and believes that he can act as he believes he ought, he would be inconsistent if he did not, in so believing, intend to act in appropriate circumstances in accord with that belief. In a word, I wish to defeat the dictum under the most favorable interpretation possible—short of defining moral sentences in such a way as to make the counter-argument self-contradictory.

There is a general condition that needs to be admitted as a

necessary condition for morally relevant discourse. If a creature is totally incapable of choice and deliberate action, he cannot in any sense be a moral agent (though this is not to say that moral judgments respecting the treatment of such a creature are not possible). It is, I think, obvious that the question whether 'ought' implies 'can,' pertains exclusively to the behavior of *agents*. Consequently, I should not deny that a moral agent is a creature capable of a considerable range of actions, choices, deliberate and intentional commitments, and the like; and, if one supposed that the dictum " 'ought' implies 'can' " were to be construed merely in this manner, I should have to admit that the dictum was entirely correct (however trivialized, on that interpretation). Those who affirm the dictum, however—prominently among them, prescriptivists—wish to hold that, distributively, for each and every possible action, it must be the case that a would-be agent of such an action must be able to perform the action if it may be claimed in a morally relevant sense that he ought to perform it. So it is that Hare, for instance, says:

> It seems to be true in general that if a description of an action is such as to rule out a practical 'Shall I?' question, then it will also rule out, for the same reason, the corresponding universally perscriptive 'Ought I?' question. It is, in fact, the impossibility of deliberating, or wondering, whether *to* do a thing which rules out asking whether one *ought* to do it.[3]

I shall take it, therefore, that if we can supply instances in which it may be said of an agent—that is, of a creature capable of a considerable range of actions, who is nevertheless incapable in a given context of performing a certain action (or not even relevantly judged with respect to his capability)—that he ought (in a moral sense) to perform that action, we shall have defeated the dictum and also decisively defeated prescriptivism, which depends on the dictum.

The first type of counter-instance, then, concerns cases in which to claim, relevantly, that someone ought to do something does not entail considerations directly of what that person can do at all. We say, for instance, that a man ought, *qua* physician, to care for, or minister to, the health of his patient—that is, in some relatively institutionalized, specified, and restricted role or capacity or function. I do not deny, as I have said, that a man must be able to do a considerable range of things if he is to be counted at all as a moral agent; nor should I deny that a man *qua* physician must be able to do a considerable range of things to be so counted. Even so, when we specify the duties of a physician, what it is that a physician ought to do in a morally relevant sense with respect to his patients, we are specifying what may be called duties of office—without regard, that is, to whether, in some quite particular case, a physician in question can or cannot fulfill his duties. In fact, if he cannot do what he ought to do, we have grounds for supposing him to be deficient with respect to his duties—which is not at all to say that he does not have these duties, that he is thereby relieved of his duties, that it is not the case that he ought to do what we say he ought to do.

This goes flatly against the prescriptivist thesis. Also, it draws our attention to an interesting distinction that is easily missed. When I say *to someone* that he ought to do such and such, I characteristically think of him as an agent sufficiently unimpeded in any relevant respect, that he can weigh my judgment and act on it if he chooses to; similarly, a man considering this or that line of action views himself as a relatively unimpeded agent. But it is perfectly possible to remind another of the duties of office that bind him (or that he may remind himself of) regardless of whether in any particular cases he can or cannot act in accord with, or to fulfill, such duties. That is, I need not view a man as, so to speak, a poised agent, a moral agent, considering what (being relatively unimpeded) he ought now to undertake to do; I may view him (and he may view himself) as a man in the role of, functioning as, physician—or, in the relationship of physician to patient—that is, *qua* physician. And, in viewing him thus, one's question respecting what he ought to do is a question of what, in general, are the duties of such an office and of what his duties are in filling his office with respect to particular patients. Since it is an independent question, in such a context, whether our physician can or cannot fulfill his duties (what it is he ought to do), I submit that it cannot be maintained that " 'ought' implies 'can' "; the question of what he ought to do, or to refrain from doing, in such and such circumstances may be raised and answered whether or not he *can* act in those circumstances. It is reasonable to hold as well —with regard to duties concerning man *qua* man (that is, distinguishing between alleged duties that may accrue to someone *qua* physician and *qua* man)—that a man, in these or those circumstances, ought not to kill; it is entirely possible to judge that he ought not, even though he be utterly incapable of killing. This is a separate question from that of whether it would be reasonable or even appropriate to *say to another* that he ought not to kill, when it is believed that the question hasn't occurred to him at all or that he is actually unable to kill. The judgment is not superfluous, though anything in the nature of a direct prescription or command or imperative or directive or warning or advice may well be superfluous. Of course, holding that 'ought' has a univocal sense in these cases, when one judges that a man has certain duties of office (or even certain duties *qua* man), we must conclude that prescriptivism and the dictum " 'ought' implies 'can' " are both untenable. But this is the weaker argument.

The second type of counter-instance concerns cases in which it is morally relevant to say of someone (or of someone to say of himself) that he ought but can't. It seems to follow directly from our first counter-argument that this must be so. For, if a physician ought (in the sense of what binds him, in his office) to do thus and such, then if he finds that he is unable to act as he ought, he can coherently say that he can't do what he knows or believes he ought to do. Hare does not deny this, I may add, though he insists that "the man who says 'I ought but I can't' . . . is [using] 'ought' in one of . . . many off-color ways that are possible." [4] The issue, one sees, depends on showing that remarks like "I ought but I can't" are not in the least off-color, do not require a "down-grading" of the moral force of 'ought.' For, it is not enough to show that if—as in our first argument—'ought' obtains without considerations of 'can,' 'ought' also obtains in the presence of 'cannot,' in the morally relevant sense. There is, then, no denial from the prescriptivist or the advocate of the dictum " 'ought' implies 'can' " that remarks like "I ought but I can't" are commonplace; the objection rather, is, that the moral sense of 'ought' has somehow been debased. Now, the classical counter-instance to the prescriptivists (as Hare very well realizes) concerns the problem of *akrasia,* or weakness of will. If *akrasia* were admitted, we should have to abandon prescriptivism as well as the dictum; and if the prescriptivist failed to interpret the problem consistently with his own view, his account would thereupon lack even minimal plausibility. For, to admit *akrasia* in its full force is to admit a morally central use of the expression "I ought but I can't."

Let me therefore, in order to facilitate our discussion, quote Hare's alternative interpretations of *akrasia,* both of which he says, though metaphorical, are "consistent with prescriptivism":

> The first is that the person who accepts some moral judgment but does not act on it is actually giving commands to himself, but unable to obey them because of a recalcitrant lower nature or 'flesh'; the other is that he is, in his whole personality or real self, ceasing to prescribe to himself (though there may be a part of him that goes on prescribing, and though he may be quite ready to prescribe to others).[5]

A rational agent, for Hare, cannot prescribe what he is not prepared to universalize, in the minimal logical or semantic sense that "we cannot without inconsistency apply a descriptive term to one thing, and refuse to apply it to another similar thing (either exactly similar or similar in the relevant respects)." [6] But by this view, the man suffering *akrasia* on the *second* interpretation cannot be a rational agent; he cannot, because he is not universalizing the alleged prescription in the relevant respects. There may well be such akrasiacs, but that is neither here nor there: what we require is a *rational* agent who shows weakness of will. The debasing of 'ought' here simply results from the agent's failure to abide by minimal considerations of consistency. (We shall return to the question of universalizability.)

The first interpretation similarly fails. For, according to Hare's view, the man showing weakness of will is said to "accept" a moral judgment or to "command" himself to act appropriately, but he is also said to be "unable to obey" the prescription given. However, if he does accept, in any relevant sense, that he ought to act in accord with a particular judgment but is unable to, then it *is* appropriate to say that he ought but can't: and if, in some sense or other, he *both* accepts and does not accept the moral judgment (metaphorically, his higher nature prescribes it and his lower nature does not), then he is not the rational agent who says that he ought but cannot. Consequently, Hare may be describing another sort of akrasiac than the one required (one with a divided self as far as "accepting" the judgment is concerned), someone who cannot, in the relevant sense, properly be said to accept a moral judgment as binding on him. There remains, nevertheless, the akrasiac who judges that he (and anyone else in similar circumstances) ought to act in such and such a way and simply cannot, is simply the victim of a weakness of will. I find no further senses in which the rational akrasiac can be denied admittance in the moral context and I must conclude, therefore, that it may be said (in a sense that is not in the least off-color) that one believes or accepts the judgment that he ought to act in such and such a way but is unable to act. But, of course, if this is possible, then it is false to hold that 'ought' implies 'can'; and it would be false to suppose that if one does not act in accord with what one apparently believes one ought to do, one simply cannot be said to believe it. Furthermore, the account converges with what we should have expected from a consideration of our first case and from our general analysis of the meaning of 'ought.'

These two sorts of cases provide a knock-down argument against the dictum " 'ought' implies 'can.' " In a sense, therefore, our argument is complete. But we may distinguish two further sorts of cases. Hare says, suggestively, "When I say 'I ought but I can't,' I am prescribing in general for cases like mine; I certainly think that a man in my situation ought, *if he can*, to do the act in question; but the prescription fails to apply in my case because of the impossibility of acting on it." [7] Consider that we are on the beach: you are an excellent swimmer and I am not; and someone is drowning in deep water and calling for help within earshot. *Since I can't* swim well, or well enough, it is not the case (accommodating the formula) that I ought to try to save the drowning swimmer; but *since you can*, you ought to. Now, if a lifeguard were near, it would be true not only that he ought to try but that he would be obliged to try (he would, because of his function, be under a distinct obligation or have a distinct duty). For men *qua* men (and not *qua* lifeguards), it is reasonable to hold that they ought, *if they can* (and only if they can), to try to save the drowning swimmer. But this consideration has to do with singling out who among possibly eligible persons ought to do what it is that ought to be done if it can be done. That is, 'if he can' serves here as a *criterion* for determining moral responsibility in special cases—where no one is under an obligation or duty of office—and not as a condition for waiving responsibility in general (or waiving the claim that one ought) whenever it is the case that one can't. *Sometimes*, it is true, it would be a mistake to claim that one ought if one can't, but it does not at all follow from this that, whenever it is the case that one can't, it ceases to be the case that one ought. We must, quite simply, distinguish the special case in question from a larger run of cases.

The second sort of case concerns ideals. Consider the following statement:

> The leader of a Himalayan expedition has the choice of either leading the final assault on the mountain himself, or staying behind at the last camp and giving another member of his party the opportunity. Here it is obvious that different ideals will conflict; yet it is easy to suppose that no argument concerned with the interests of the parties will settle the question—for the interests may be very precisely balanced. The questions that arise are likely to be concerned, not with the interests of the parties, but with ideals of what a man should *be*. Is it better to be the sort of man who, in face of great obstacles and dangers, gets to the top of the nth highest mountain in the world; or the sort of man who uses his position of authority to give a friend this opportunity instead of claiming it for himself? These questions are very like aesthetic ones. It is as if a man were regarding his own life and character as a work of art, and asking how it should best be completed.[8]

I wish to distinguish the question indicated from another closely related one. I can well imagine claiming (holding to this or that ideal) that another ought to live according to a given ideal. And I am prepared to concede, in saying that disputes about ideals are like aesthetic quarrels, that one would not judge that so and so ought to live in accord with a certain ideal unless he believed that he could. Ideals do not correspond with duties of office and the like, although philosophers like Plato and Kant often talk as if man *qua* man had a function or an office to fulfill; if they were right, talk about such ideals would reduce to talk about duties of office, but then our earlier arguments would be decisive here as well. Still, because ideals do not concern established functions and roles (ideals regarding man *qua* man) and because they correspond to alternative ways of appreciating or construing the possibilities of human life, it is probably the case that we do not say to anyone that he ought to act in accord with a given ideal unless we believe that he can. That is, the only sense in which we judge a man relative to ideals that may be adopted is the sense in which he is what I have called a poised agent—which is of course fully compatible with the dictum " 'ought' implies 'can.' "

However, to claim that a man ought to act in this or that way, in order to act in accord with some preferred ideal, is not the same as claiming that the ideal itself ought to prevail. There is a difference between making moral claims about what a man should do and, following the terms of reference of the Himalayan illustration, making moral claims about what a man should *be*. The claim, for example, that men ought to be ascetic may be construed equivocally—as holding that men ought to do whatever would accord with the ascetic ideal or as holding that the ascetic life is the ideal life for man. On the first interpretation, I concede that the dictum " 'ought' implies 'can' " would not be threatened at all. But on the second, inasmuch as the moral judgment would have to be construed as an appreciative judgment of some sort—and Hare, speaking to this very issue, concedes that "it is impossible, and moral philosophers ought not to try, to find methods of argument which will settle, determinately, disputes between upholders of different ideals in all cases" [9]—the dictum would fall and prescriptivism would fail. Consequently, if disputes about alternative ideals are admitted to be morally relevant and if to claim that man ought *to be* ascetic, for instance, is to make a moral claim about a particular ideal among possible competitors, then even if it were true that one would not say to another that he ought to act in accord with such an ideal unless he were a poised agent, the judgment of what man ought to be could not be readily construed as supporting the dictum that 'ought' implies 'can' or that moral judgments are essentially prescriptive. If 'ought' may be used in appreciative judgments regarding morally relevant ideals of life, then, clearly, for a special (but not unimportant) range of cases, prescriptivism and the dictum " 'ought' implies 'can' " would fall. And if 'ought' may be used thus, then assuming a univocal sense of 'ought,' to judge what it is that a man ought to do (as distinct from *telling* him to do what he ought to do, or the like) is to judge that he falls under a certain condition or rule or principle (for instance, that a certain course of action is relevantly ranked as superior to all alternative courses of action—independently of considerations of what, in the interval referred to in the judgment, he can do). And if this is the case, then at least a large range of moral judgments may well be characterizable as descriptive rather than prescriptive (excluding, of course, appreciative judgments, which fail to be either prescriptive or descriptive) without denying that one may, in issuing a moral judgment, intend to direct another to act in a certain way.

There is, however, an extremely important detail, to which we have alluded, that needs to be analyzed here in order to round out our account. We have seen that the argument regarding *akrasia* requires speaking of a rational akrasiac, one who exhibits weakness of will at the same time that he universalizes the moral judgment to which he subscribes. Hare, who holds that moral judgments "share *one* important characteristic with imperatives, that of being prescriptive," [10] holds also "that [moral prescriptives] are distinguished from other judgments of this class by being *universalizable*." [11] The difficulties facing imperativism and the thesis that moral judgments are action-guiding have already been sufficiently explicated. It remains merely to show that this additional restriction, that of universalizability, is trivial and useless; and also that it may, in a critical respect, be confused with an equally empty but quite different principle of a morally relevant sort. The issue is quickly resolved.

Hare says, quite rightly, that "the thesis that descriptive judgments are universalizable is a quite trivial thesis"; for, as he explains, "any singular descriptive judgment is universalizable . . . in the sense that it commits the speaker to the further proposition that anything exactly like the subject of the first judgment, or like it in relevant respects, possesses the property attributed to it in the first judgment." He holds, paradoxically, that moral judgments are *"in the same sense,* universalizable" but that that thesis "is itself not so trivial." [12] He means that moral judgments have descriptive properties but are not merely descriptive judgments and that universalizability holds even though they are prescriptive judgments. It may be argued, however (to dramatize the triviality of the thesis for both descriptive and prescriptive judgments), that even singular imperatives may be construed as universalizable but that the relevant respect in which they are, concerns solely the unit class of subjects addressed by the singular imperative. Thus, whoever is "exactly like the subject of the first" imperative (there being none other) is addressed by the further imperative to which one is committed in committing himself to the original singular imperative. At the very least, then, moral judgments construed as prescriptives could not be marked off from imperatives by virtue of the formal property of universalizability. Obviously, the alleged distinction, if defensible, would have allowed a somewhat Kantian-like demarcation of distinctive kinds of judgments—an achievement incompatible with our own analysis of value judgments.

To the principle of universalizability, there corresponds "a descriptive meaning-rule," from the applicability of which (as Hare says) it is "a direct consequence . . . that we cannot without inconsistency apply a descriptive term to one thing, and refuse to apply it to another similar thing (either exactly similar or similar in the relevant respects)." [13] This makes it quite clear that universalizability is a *logical thesis* and not a moral thesis. "By a 'logical' thesis" is meant "a thesis about the meanings of words, or dependent solely upon them": the meaning of 'ought' and similar words "is such that a person who uses them commits himself thereby to a universal rule"—which is simply "the thesis of universalizability." [14] I put this as carefully as I can because of an obvious source of equivocation here. For, when he first introduces the concept of universalizability, Hare says that "it is, most fundamentally, because moral judgments are universalizable that we can speak of moral thought as rational (to universalize is to give the reason). . . ." [15] But, if to universalize is to give the (morally relevant) reason, then the principle of universalizability is a moral principle and not (or not merely) a logical principle; and if the principle is solely concerned with meanings, it cannot be a moral principle.

The issue is troublesome largely because of a possible confusion respecting the role of proper names and references to particular times and places and persons in universalized formulas.[16] (We shall return to this issue in another context.) But the general trouble concerns conflating the logical principle of universalizability and the moral principle of generality. Both are quite vacant but are supplied content in quite different ways: universalizability requires some semantic commitments over which it ranges; generality concerns the range or extension of cases over which particular and different moral rules obtain. Consequently, generality is given content by some substantive *moral* principle or criterion. The judgment that X is a murderer, considered in terms of universalizability, draws attention only to consistency of usage; but considered in terms of generality, it draws attention to some criterion or principle or rule in terms of which the case at stake is seen to fall within the scope of what we call murder. Universalizability concerns consistent usage respecting relevant resemblances admitted, and generality concerns the actual specification of relevant resemblances. It is in this sense that it is impossible (*pace* Kant) to provide a satisfactory moral criterion or principle that is purely formal. Universalizability cannot determine the moral relevance of particular restrictions of generality with respect to given moral principles and rules; and the principle of generality is entirely vacant without some moral commitment with respect to which the *relevance* of runs of similarities and differences may be determined and cases codified. This is why, for instance, Kant was obliged to introduce teleological considerations with respect to which the Categorical Imperative was to function. It makes no difference, in a purely formal sense, whether one is a eudaimonist, an egoist, or a utilitarian with respect to accepting the principle of generality: *some* such commitment is required in order to escape the vacuity of the principle itself.

The confusion at stake happens to be rather clearly illustrated by Hare's discussion. Consider the following, for instance:

> When we are trying, in a concrete case, to decide what we ought to do, what we are looking for . . . is an action to which we can commit ourselves (prescriptively) but which we are at the same time prepared to accept as exemplifying a principle of action to be prescribed for others in like circumstances (universalizability). If, when we consider some proposed action, we find that, when universalized, it yields prescriptions which we cannot accept, we reject this action as a solution to our moral problem—if we cannot universalize the prescription, it cannot become an 'ought.' [17]

If universalizability were merely a logical principle, no self-consistent moral proposal could be rejected by appealing to it. But when Hare speaks of our being "prepared to accept" the universalized proposal or says that "we cannot universalize the prescription," he must be converting universalizability into a moral rule: *he must be speaking of rejecting a particular moral proposal of some generality.* That *that* proposal must be universalizable (if self-consistent) is, as we have seen, entirely trivial. Hence, it is simply a mistake to hold, for example, that " 'ought'-judgments have to be universalizable, which, in the strict sense, legal judgments are not." [18] It is also a mistake to hold that "the universalist is committed to a denial of relativism" (at least for the reason alleged);[19] for if one takes relativism to be concerned with the existence of changing and different moral convictions, then it cannot be the case that the universalist opposes relativism—*his* contribution is strictly limited to considerations of logical and semantic consistency. The upshot of our insistence, then, is that all substantive questions regarding *what* it is we ought or ought not to do (an analogous argument could of course be formulated for 'good' and 'right' and other allied terms) are left unaffected by the analysis of the meaning of 'ought' or of the condition of universalizability.

Seen from a larger point of view, what we are confirming is the importance of an ethically neutral analysis of 'ought' and the ease with which substantive partisan convictions pretend to be derived from metaethical analyses. To some extent, these same issues are involved in assessing the doctrine " 'ought' cannot be derived from 'is' "—which of course is merely a special case of the general doctrine that evaluative statements cannot be derived from descriptive statements.

Again, we may cite a remark of Hare's in order to facilitate our inquiry. Hare holds that "all words which are evaluative . . . are also prescriptive; but there are expressions which are prescriptive but not evaluative (because they do not carry descriptive meaning as well)." [20] The trouble here is compound. For one thing, as we have seen, prescriptivism is indefensible as a comprehensive theory of moral judgments; *a fortiori* indefensible for the entire range of value judgments; for another, even 'ought'-judgments are not uniformly action-guiding; for a third, the distinction between evaluative and non-evaluative statements depends on the predicates employed and not on whether such statements or judgments may be true or false or correct or incorrect; for a fourth, although *words* may be evaluative, only *sentences* used in certain specifiable ways are prescriptive; and for a fifth, 'ought' used in a univocal sense in a range of statements sometimes appears in utterances that are prescriptive, sometimes not. But if we eliminate prescriptivism and even prescriptive (or commendatory or emotive) utterances, we are faced, in assessing the doctrine " 'ought' cannot be derived from 'is,' " solely with the question whether statements employing valuational predicates can be derived from statements employing non-valuational predicates (in whatever way arguments may be constructed for statements employing non-valuational predicates only). Once the issue is thus construed, one sees both the irrelevance of most objections and the obvious validity of arguments of the required form. Simply grant that certain valuational predicates are extensionally equivalent to certain non-valuational predicates or that certain non-valuational attributes count as evidence for the presence of certain valuational attributes, and precisely the same logical connections admitted to hold for statements employing non-valuational predicates will hold in arguments involving statements that employ valuational predicates. The argument is incontrovertible: from the fact that he has won certain contests, it is, for instance, logically possible to conclude that one is the best contender; from the fact that he has taken another's life in a certain way under certain circumstances, it is logically possible to conclude that one is a murderer or has done what he ought not to have done. Such arguments are utterly unexceptional, *once* one sees that cognitivism is not at stake nor any theory of the nature of the external world. It will still be possible, as has already been shown, that the distinction between value judgments and non-value judgments can be maintained on the basis of the theoretical role of valuational predicates in our conceptual network.

The only interesting issue concerns the *kind* of fact that is stated in an evaluative statement, but this is not in any way prejudiced by upsetting the doctrine " 'ought' cannot be derived from 'is.' " We can, therefore, subscribe to John Searle's sketch, for instance, of all such arguments:

> I started with a brute fact, that a man uttered certain words ["I hereby promise to pay you, Smith, five dollars"], and

then invoked the institution [of promising] in such a way
as to generate institutional facts [that Jones, who promised,
placed himself under an obligation] by which we arrived at
the conclusion that, as regards his obligation, the man ought
to pay another man five dollars.[21]

The interesting question concerns the analysis of so-called "institutional facts." Searle himself holds that, probably, "no set of
brute fact statements can entail an institutional fact statement
without the addition of at least one constitutive rule," [22] but this
is merely to postpone the issue; for we will inevitably have to
press on to determine whether there *are,* and in what sense there
are, constitutive rules, which are morally binding. Here, the difference between moral and non-moral values—to which we have
already referred—is crucial. Given values that are *not* overriding,
it is relatively easy to concede that there are institutional facts
answering to temporary, contingent, even idiosyncratic interests;
and given such institutional facts, it is relatively easy to admit
arguments in which evaluative conclusions are derived from descriptive premises. Given a general interest, for instance, in
the institutions of baseball and boxing, it is easy to determine
whether a batter or a fighter is "out." But, precisely where the
values are overriding values (moral values), the required institutional facts or "constitutive rules" cannot merely be conceded
to answer to certain interests—they are just what the quarrel is
about—and, consequently, although, *given* certain descriptive
premises, it must be admitted that (morally) evaluative conclusions may be derived from such premises, the ulterior question remains, the question concerning the sense in which *such*
premises hold and *such* conclusions are binding on moral
agents. This is a matter that cannot be answered by any merely
logical or semantical inquiry.

The upshot of this is extremely important. For, conceding the
difference between the conditional and overriding values of,
respectively, non-moral and moral interests, it is an inherently

partisan move—in fact, a morally conservative move—to hold that "anyone who uses [the] word ['promise'] in serious literal speech is committed to its logical consequences involving obligations . . . that, in the case of certain institutional facts, the evaluations involving obligations, commitments, and responsibilities are no longer left completely open because the statement of the institutional facts involves these notions" (a thesis that may be termed "crypto-cognitivism").[23] Alternatively put, it is quite impossible "to make a distinction between what is external and what is internal to the institution of promising"[24] (construed as a moral and not a merely linguistic institution, that is, as embodying overriding values) in any way analogous to making such a distinction respecting mere linguistic institutions or other non-moral institutional facts. The reason is quite simple: on the view at issue, one could never say both that he *understands* the sense in which "accepting" the institution of promising (and using 'promise' correctly) places him under a certain obligation *and* that he does not acknowledge such obligations as binding on himself. The problem is that one cannot assume that speaking in accord with certain linguistic conventions itself entails "accepting" (in whatever sense one may provide) the overriding values putatively embedded in established linguistic usage; consequently, it is quite misleading to suppose that "serious literal speech" commits one morally, and not merely linguistically, to certain institutions. To derive 'ought' from 'is' is a strictly linguistic matter; to confuse the linguistic and the moral is to fail to allow that critics of a given institution may be "internal" and not merely "external" critics—both in terms of membership in a linguistic community and in terms of membership in a moral community.[25] But this is simply to confirm again the ease with which substantive and partisan doctrines may masquerade as neutral metaethical doctrines.

CHAPTER 5

'Good,' 'Right,' 'Duty'

THERE IS EVERY REASON to suppose that, having provided a univocal sense of 'ought' ranging over both moral and non-moral discourse, we can provide as well a corresponding analysis of such key terms as 'good' ('bad'), 'right' ('wrong'), 'duty' ('rights'), 'obligatory' ('forbidden,' 'permissible'), and the like. The account required should, at one and the same time, preserve a neutrality regarding substantive moral convictions and detail whatever systematic relationships hold among such terms. This is, of course, not to ignore a host of other important terms—for instance, 'courageous,' 'humane,' 'decent,' 'saintly,' 'evil,' 'horrible,' 'admirable,' 'nice,' 'pleasant,' 'happy,' 'just,' 'fair,' 'reasonable.' But the analysis of the key terms promises to integrate the principal directions of ethical concern and to allow, in a systematic way, for refinement and detail. In fact, sanguine expectations of a somewhat related sort have lead to such classical metamoral doctrines as, that what is right is determined by what is good (for instance, utilitarianism), that what is right is what accords with duty or obligation independently of considerations of goodness (for instance, Kant's doctrine), and that what is morally good is determined by what is right or is only contingently connected with what is right (for instance the views of deontologists like H. A. Prichard and W. D. Ross).

These doctrines pose an obvious dilemma; for, if they have any currency, seemingly neutral metaethical analysis will "discover" that there is indeed some evidence supporting the relevant "linguistic" thesis; on the other hand, there appears to be no way to fix the semantic relationships among these terms that cannot itself be made to favor one or another of the corresponding metamoral doctrines. The upshot is that the only objective metaethical thesis that can be provided here is tantamount simply to an admission of this very connection between linguistic usage and moral conviction. For instance, Kantian-like moral agents and critics, conceding that there may well be some benefit, some good, yielded in doing one's duty, will nevertheless insist that such consequences cannot decide or affect the essential moral question whether one is acting rightly or acting as one ought or in accord with one's obligation; and, given their moral convictions and a linguistic practice consistent with them, any "independent" metaethical inquiry that does not disregard such practice will confirm that there are indeed linguistic grounds for the Kantian position! But if this is so, then no such partisan metamoral thesis can hope—contrary to the spirit of a great many traditional quarrels—to establish its particular claims on the basis of linguistic usage, usage that can be made to accommodate as well the incompatible claims of competing metamoral theories. W. D. Ross, for instance, argues (in considering what makes keeping a promise right), "that no one *means* by 'right' just 'productive of the best possible consequences,' or 'optimific.'"[1] Of course, a utilitarian of some sort (an act-utilitarian, as he would now be called—for instance, J. J. C. Smart) might *mean* by 'right,' 'optimific.'[2] Ross counters this possibility, arguing that we would not normally suppose it to be open to someone to decide whether, for instance, to keep a particular promise on the basis of the anticipated balance of good and bad consequences; and he goes on to say "that there is no self-evident connection between the attributes 'right' and 'optimific' . . . [that] the coextensiveness of the right and the optimific is . . . not self-evident," and that their synonymy or equivalence cannot be established by any straightforward deductive or inductive means. But to say these things demonstrates only that there is *some* linguistic support (perhaps even invented to accommodate the underlying metamoral theory) for Ross' view, without at all foreclosing on utilitarianism or its characteristic usage. On merely linguistic grounds, then, all such metamoral theories are false, since if they have advocates no competing theory can fail to be disconfirmed on the strength of *their* usage! But this is simply to establish the inadequacy of purely linguistic methods for deciding the substantive issues.

The best strategy that we may adopt, then, in testing any particular metaethical theory of the relevant sort, is to propose counter-instances that the advocate in question is bound to admit; for this permits us both to assess the scope and internal coherence of any theory and to dramatize the intimate conceptual connection between metamoral convictions and linguistic usage. Thus, we may conditionally admit a certain range of moral data for purposes of testing and, at the same time, admit the possibility that the data in question may be quite differently construed from the vantage of some alternative metamoral theory. We may, then, proceeding in this way, map relatively comprehensive and alternative relationships among the key ethical terms without subscribing to any particular substantive theory.

Thus, when he turns "to consider the nature of individual right acts," taking the famous instance of having promised to return a book to a friend, Ross inadvertently and without sufficient grounds turns instead to speak of "our duty, our duty to fulfill our promise, i.e. to put the book into our friend's possession." What we need to see is that Ross has here conflated a substantive view about *what* we are committed to in making a promise and a metaethical thesis about the relationship between 'right' and 'duty.' We may see this merely by considering Ross' curious thesis, in speaking of keeping a promise, that "success and failure are the only test, and a sufficient test, of the performance of duty."

For one thing, it does not at all follow from my having promised to return a book that, though I have thereby contracted a *prima facie* duty, I have contracted a duty *sans phrase;* nor does it follow from my having promised to return a book that my duty is not fulfilled unless I have "put the book into [my] friend's possession." Sometimes, my duty, as often in contracts and promises, is not fulfilled unless "success" of the sort Ross has in mind is achieved and, sometimes, my duty is fulfilled if I have tried to do what I have promised or contracted to do (that is, if I succeed with respect to trying), even when I fail to do what I thereby intend to do. If, for instance, I contract to return a book borrowed from the public library and the book is lost in the mails (and this can be established), it is not clear that I have failed, in failing to return the book, to fulfill my duty (which, it seems, was to make all reasonable effort to return the book, as far as it was in my power to do so). And if I promise to meet you at a certain time at a certain place, I have (normally) fulfilled my duty (the duty contracted *by* the promise) in trying in every reasonable way to meet you. But if I have an automobile accident on the way and am thus prevented from meeting you, I have (in an allowable sense) still fulfilled the duty I contracted, in having tried—however true it may be that I have failed to meet you. The excuse I should provide would show that I lived up to my promise, though I did not succeed in doing what, in doing what I promised, I had intended thereby to do. I promised to meet you, intending to meet you; I failed to meet you but I succeeded in fulfilling my promise, that is, I tried in every reasonable way to meet you at the place and time appointed. (This is, obviously, a substantive ethical issue, highly debatable, and open to competing plausible assessments.) If, on the other hand, I contract to pay a certain debt, it is probably the case that only the payment of the debt will fulfill my duty, that (normally) my trying (but failing) will not fulfill my contract or my duty. Ross is mistaken, therefore, in thinking that promises and contracts, which *do* generate duties, generate duties of one sort only. He may be mistaken also in supposing that whenever I promise, I put myself under an obligation or accept a duty (as distinct from it merely being the case that if I promise to X, I *ought* to X); for instance, I may promise to come to your party. But if I don't, have I failed in my *duty*? "Am I immoral?" [3] But Ross is perhaps most seriously mistaken in thinking that "individual right acts" are acts that, as such, concern doing one's duty. The point is that the substantive moral issue is debatable and that alternative connections between 'right' and 'duty' are eligible on the basis of the very range of putative data on which Ross relies.

Consider that, even if I should fulfill my duty to return, or to try to return, a book to a friend *by* "the packing and posting of [the] book," it would (normally) be no part of my duty to pack and post it. Sometimes, duties are detailed about how things of this sort should be handled, but often not. What I did, in packing and posting the book, was a right action relative to fulfilling my promise; but I could easily have returned the book (or tried to) in a variety of ways, and all of these might have been *right* or *all right* or *equally right* relative to my duty. Here, Ross has fallen victim to an important equivocation about right and duty. For, we say both that it is right (or good) to do one's duty and that it is one's duty to do what is right (or good); and these by no means come to the same thing.

When I say that one has a duty to do what is right, I surely cannot mean to say that one has a duty to do *whatever* is right (or even whatever is morally right), that is, whatever in given circumstances could (by any view of 'right') be reasonably construed as right. (A corresponding argument, of course, may be constructed for 'good.') If I were to say, for instance, that it would be right (even morally right) to ventilate coal mines more effectively, it by no means follows that I or anyone else have a duty to ventilate those coal mines. Or, to take a more suggestive case, if to give a certain answer on a test is to do what is right relative to that test, or to do one's work right, it by no means follows that anyone taking the test has a duty to give the right answer. No, when we say that one has a duty to do what is right, we mean: to do what is right *rather than what is wrong,* where choice is possible and relevant. But considerations of right and wrong often obtain when no questions of duty arise at all. Doing what is right is not, as such, doing one's duty. On the other hand, when we say that it is right to do our duty, we are perhaps drawing attention to the fact that whatever is our duty, is, as such, right to do, that its being one's duty entails its being right for one to do.

At this point, it becomes extremely helpful to insist on the univocity of 'right' for a very wide range of cases that include, but are not restricted to, the moral domain. I see no reason for thinking (paralleling our discussion of 'ought') that 'right,' in expressions like 'right answer' with respect to an arithmetic test, 'right road' for a path to a predetermined goal, 'right treatment' with respect to some respiratory ailment to be treated, 'right impression' to characterize actions effective in persuading a client to make a purchase, 'right thing to do' to characterize either supererogatory kindness or what etiquette indicates or what one is obliged to do—I say I see no reason for saying that 'right'—is not being used univocally. In all of these and similar instances, 'right' appears to mean 'appropriate,' 'proper,' 'acceptable,' 'correct,' 'admissible,' 'permissible,' and the like, with respect to relatively formalized or professionalized or institutionalized practices having fairly explicit norms. The respect in which something is right will, of course, vary from context to context and, consequently, the criteria for judging that something is right will vary from context to context. 'Right,' it seems, rather like 'ought,' always has to do with human action and expectation, though it is perhaps possible to call something right that is not, narrowly, an action or expectation. The right answer to an arithmetic problem is whatever rightly solves the problem, there being perhaps alternative solutions (even if not alternative values) for the problem. The right road to take from A to B is whatever road, within implied limits, takes one from A to B, with attention to comfort, distance, safety, directness, and the like (though there may well be alternative roads that are equally right or as right as any other to take). If I have a duty to return, or to try to return, a friend's book, I will have fulfilled my duty in *the* right way or in *a* way that is right if the means I select meet the criteria imposed by my duty. According to this view, then, to say that it is right to do my duty is to say that it is (always) appropriate, proper, correct to do my duty with respect to a given moral or legal or military code or the like: if the duty is a *prima facie* duty, then to act thus will be *prima facie* right. But, once again, I may well do what is right without it being my duty to do it.

One sees, at a stroke, that *if* 'right' is univocal for the wide range of contexts indicated, it is impossible to hold that doing what is right is doing what is one's duty (or one's obligation or what one ought to do). The reason is simply that, in a very large number of cases, questions of duty and the like do not arise at all. The question of what is the right card to play at a particular point in a bridge game does not raise, as such, a question of duty (though given that a certain move is *the* right or *a* right play *and given* that one is committed to winning the game, one ought relevantly to prefer that move to any that is wrong—which, again, has nothing to do with duty or obligation). Furthermore, even in a moral context, if I befriend you at a party in order to make you comfortable, I may have done what, in terms of friendliness and hospitality, is the right, or a right, thing to do or what is all right to do: it may, that is, be proper or appropriate or permissible, but it need not, for that reason, be obligatory or in any sense a duty. The very tripartite division of the obligatory, the forbidden, and the permissible vouchsafes the thesis, for the permissible is, precisely, what is neither obligatory nor forbidden, what duty does not require. In fact, in characterizing an act as the right thing to do, one is, often, not characterizing it as the only right thing to do: given the circumstances, it may well be the only right possibility as yet formulated or may merely be preferable to others that are up to that moment formulated. Also, duties are ascribed to persons (either particular persons or whoever may be) in certain roles, functions, and the like; what are right are certain actions, expectations, arrangements, and the like in suitably institutionalized or formalized settings. Consequently, sometimes things may be judged to be right (for instance, proportions) without assuming that anyone is actually committed to fulfilling any relevant role or function or relationship.

Here, then, we may jump to a rather large generalization. I should claim that 'right' ('wrong') and 'good' ('bad') are—granting always that value judgments may be findings, that is, in the indicative mood and capable of being true and false—*grading* predicates, whereas 'obligatory,' 'duty,' and 'ought' are *ranking* predicates. To say that something is right rather than wrong is to say that it passes a certain test or criterion or qualification but not that it is preeminent or takes precedence in any respect (except, precisely, over what is wrong); but to say that something is obligatory or forbidden or the like is to say that it ranks highest or lowest among a set of relevant alternatives for action (not merely in moral contexts but also, perhaps, in the context of games or other specialized interests). Consequently, we see why it is that it is right to do one's duty: the preeminent alternative for action is, at the very least, a proper alternative for action. But we cannot say that one has a duty to do whatever is right, meaning whatever may be judged right in a given context, for we cannot infer that whatever is appropriate or permissible is, for that reason, also obligatory or that what is permissible is in any sense preeminent. Also, if one believes that a given act is (morally) what he ought to do or is his duty or obligation under the circumstances, then he cannot, consistently with his belief, not intend thus to act if he believes he is capable of so acting; for the judgment is a ranking of alternatives concerning overriding values. But if a man merely believes that a given act would be right or all right to do, under the circumstances, considerably more latitude obtains respecting consistency between belief and action; for here, he is merely grading alternatives respecting overriding values. The point counts seriously against prescriptivism.

Now, insofar as there are reasons and interests for grading things as right and wrong, there are, quite often, consequences that follow on such grading, depending on the context and criteria of grading—*a fortiori*, there will be corresponding consequences for ranking as well. But it must be emphasized that these may always be distinguished from the judgments themselves. Thus, for instance, if an answer to an arithmetic test is judged wrong, one's grade may be correspondingly lowered. In general, there are separable penalties that follow upon the judgment of something's being wrong; and, in general, either there are rewards that follow upon judging something to be right or, at least, there is escape from some relevant penalty. The formality and informality of such penalties and similar considerations are of no concern here. It is sufficient to note that, *if* 'right' and 'wrong' are univocal for the range indicated, then it is (trivially) a mistake to think that 'wrong' is always a term of censure or reproach or blame. If one makes a wrong move in chess, one forfeits a piece, but there is no censure entailed. Similarly, if one parks in a no-parking zone, one may be fined (that is, penalized), though he may be invited to pay his fine by mail (which is to say, he is not being punished or reproached or censured in any way). It is, of course, quite possible to punish someone by fine or forfeit or penalty, but it does not follow that all cases of penalty (where actions are relevantly detected to be wrong) are cases of punishment or censure or reproach. If a baseball player insults the umpire, he may be punished by fine and penalty, but though the team may be penalized by losing his services for the game or period, the team itself is by no means thereby being punished.

The interesting thing is that it seems rather more difficult, in the moral context, to separate the judgment that one's action is wrong from punishment, censure, reproach, blame, and the like.

The reason, of course, is that morality concerns overriding values. Punishment, however, at least in its full-blown sense, is a very complex practice that is called into play only with some relatively formalized or institutionalized relationship or office of some sort (fathers with respect to children, courts with respect to criminals), unless (what is not altogether unreasonable) censure and reproach and blame are themselves construed as punishment—where these notions are taken to cover the deliberate inflicting of hurt or pain or harm or the deprivation of some benefit or advantage, deemed justified on the grounds that the wrong action done is in some measure reprehensible or blameworthy.

To judge that someone acted wrongly, in the moral context, does seem regularly to imply that he acted reprehensibly or in a way that is to be condemned or censured or noted for reproach or blame. If, however, reproach and punishment and the like require *addressing* the agent thus judged, even if only addressing the judgment to him, then, clearly, the judgment that someone acted wrongly does not entail punishment, censure, reproach, condemnation, blame, or the like. But if to censure or to blame is merely to mark what deserves punishment or the like or would justify addressing an agent with an adverse judgment, then, quite trivially, judging that someone has acted wrongly *is* censuring or reproaching him; but then, it cannot be construed as inflicting any hurt or disadvantage as in the manner of punishment. Also, the reason for the intimate link between judging that one has acted wrongly and reproach is not far to seek. For, as we have seen, even with respect to what is not strictly our duty, we are said (analytically) to have a duty to prefer what is right to what is wrong; this is true, in general, for rational agents and, *a fortiori,* it is true for moral agents in moral contexts. So a double criticism is possible: it is right to do one's duty—and doing what is wrong may go against one's explicit duty; and one has a duty, morally speaking, to do what is right (that is, to do what is opposed to what is wrong). The second alternative may be read as trivializing the sense in which a rational agent has duties; the first merely assumes that he has duties.

Still, if 'wrong' is univocal across the range of contexts we have already considered, then—apart from the contingency of punishment and censure and reproach—censure and blame depend on the criteria on which the relevant moral (or quasi-moral) judgments rest and also on ulterior concerns of moral practice rather than on the mere sense of 'wrong' itself. In the setting of an arithmetic test, a wrong answer is simply one that is inadmissible or incorrect; the penalty involved, if any, is something like a loss of grade. But it is altogether possible to provide a wrong answer without suffering any penalty (let alone punishment), unless merely being wrong itself is a penalty (or else the implied lack of power or skill or attention), which is altogether unconvincing. In the moral context, one may judge in his heart that what he has done is wrong. His penalty here may be a sense of guilt, which, considered as self-reproach, may even be taken to constitute a kind of punishment. But the judgment and these consequences are only contingently connected, however appropriate in practice the passage from the one to the other may be. Also, what a man has done may have been wrong, in the sense that had he been more perceptive, he would not have acted thus; but he may not, in so acting, have acted wrongly with respect to motives and beliefs and the like. Here, it appears, we should be content to note, surely without censure or blame or punishment, that his choice or decision, though fully morally significant, was the wrong one to make.[4] On the other hand, remorse and a sense of guilt or an active conscience are simply affective counterparts of our judging the consistency of belief and action. They may, therefore, be themselves assessed for accuracy and the like, as may our judgments. Otherwise, they will be construed cognitively, which is at least premature.

We may collect these distinctions more systematically. 'Right,' relative to all valuational contexts, is a univocal grading term, the predicative use of which depends on criteria appropriate to different contexts. Relative to such contexts, different questions of penalty and punishment and their analogues obtain, though contingent upon ulterior practical interests. 'Right' does not have the same meaning as 'good' nor the meaning of 'duty' nor are the conceptual connections among these terms altogether simple and straightforward. 'Duty' (also, 'obligatory' and 'ought') is, by contrast with 'right,' a ranking term respecting what takes precedence among all relevant alternatives of action—primarily bearing on what is required by one's office or function or relationship (as being citizen, father, policeman, or priest); consequently, rational belief about what one's duty is and the like (as opposed to belief about what is right or all right to do) entails the intention of acting accordingly, on the condition of believing that one is able to act thus—conditionally on one's interests, in non-moral contexts; categorically, in the moral context. But also, what it is one's duty to do (or what is obligatory or what one ought to do) is also right to do: what is, on any criterion, the preeminent alternative is at least (trivially) a permissible alternative; but the converse, clearly, does not hold. Furthermore, we may say, if 'good' is, as it appears to be, a grading term and if to use the term is to predicate merit or worth or value of something, then whatever is right is, at least minimally, good: whatever is appropriate or correct or acceptable or admissible or permissible possesses, as such, some merit—is, as Ross would say, at least "bonific." But what is good need not be what is right, simply because the merit to be assigned may not concern formalized or institutionalized practices or any practices at all. 'Good' is the most general grading term that we have—suitable for every evaluative occasion. This is why, incidentally, so many metamoral theories that appear to urge, in one way or another, that we maximize goodness are utterly trivial: if they cannot be denied, they are analytically true; and if they are not analytically true, it is not clear that they are, or in what sense they are, true at all.

Questions of duty, then, and of obligation and of what one ought to do concern deliberate action; similarly, questions of what is right. Questions of what is good need not but may concern actions. Predications of goodness range over an enormous run of heterogeneous items, over whatever may be judged in terms of rightness and duty and more: men, their actions, their characters, their intentions, their abilities, their thoughts, their satisfactions, their appearances, their condition, their influence, their relations, and the like are all said to be good in one respect or another; and things, events, arrangements, both natural and artificial, are said to be good in different ways.[5] Also, the clichés of moral philosophy cannot be denied: what is wrong may have good consequences and what is right, bad consequences; and if this is true, *a fortiori*, it is true of duties and obligations. What is good need not be right; and what is right, though it does concern actions, need not correspond to one's duty. On the other hand, what is one's duty is (analytically) right to do, and what is right possesses (analytically) some measure of goodness. If "It is right to do one's duty" and "It is good to do what is right" are construed analytically, then it is trivial, in particular instances, to insist, as with Ross, that doing one's duty or what is right is bonific.

The serious question raised by large-scale utilitarian and deontological theories concerns rather how to justify ethical doctrines like, "One ought only to maximize goodness," or "What is good is morally justified only if it accords with what is right or with doing one's duty," or "Considerations of goodness are irrelevant to judging what is right or what one's duty is." The interesting thing, given the foregoing analysis, is that no such doctrine is in the least degree distinctly and preferentially supported by metaethical inquiry.

Nevertheless, the counter-thesis dies slowly and, short of subscribing to some global metamoral theory or other, writers occupied with metaethical issues pretend to discern, in the very meaning of 'good' and related terms, crucial and substantive consequences affecting the determination of normative values; and this, despite the fact that, distinguishing the sense and criteria of use of all such terms, the formal relations among them would appear to yield nothing decisive. The issue cannot be put to rest without attention to the claims of moral cognitivism, though it appears—as we have already seen—in the guise of neutral metaethical views. Thus, as Searle claims, using moral terms "in serious literal speech" entails being committed to the moral institutions such use "involves." But one may always construe such commitments as conditional on particular interests (call them "moral" or "conventional" if you will) and reserve another sign for the distinction of overriding values (call them "truly moral" or "real" or "genuine" if you will). The point is that if a merely linguistic argument is alleged to fix our overriding values, we can also, also by linguistic means, deny the claim consistently with usage. So there is a stalemate here. But we should expose as well the inherent weakness of the relevant theories.

Stuart Hampshire, for example, holds that "the notion of goodness . . . necessarily enters into every kind of discourse in which statements can be made":[6]

> We necessarily have the idea of "more or less a so-and-so" as part of the procedure of classification itself, and therefore as intrinsic to any use of language in thought and in speech.

Hampshire's point is that "anyone who applies concepts necessarily applies also the distinction between a standard or normal case of something falling under a concept and an abnormal or imperfect case." If he were correct in this, it would follow that "good so-and-so" (or an equivalent) would necessarily be provided for in any language merely in having provided for the use of classifying concepts; and classifying concepts, Hampshire argues, are themselves inescapable.[7] But the thesis is untenable.

The idea of "more or less a so-and-so" appears to have a quite restricted and not unavoidable use. For instance, in standard cases of classification, in classifying tigers, lions, tapirs, there seems to be no obvious need to speak of "more or less a so-and-so." We should, I think, find it more inescapable to speak of something's being "more or less *like* a so-and-so." The difference is instructive. Because the clearest conceivable sense (though not the only one) in which we might (or might be forced to) speak of something being "more or less a so-and-so," where the comment is taken to be a *classifying* remark, would be that in which we were speaking of fixed species, of classes to which definable essences might be assigned. In such a setting, to say that X is, say, "less a so-and-so" *is* to indicate that X is "an abnormal or imperfect case." But if we do not have fixed species (and Hampshire's discussion rejects any claim that there are such), it is not immediately obvious that classification entails provision for "the notion of goodness" (or for "the idea of 'more or less a so-and-so' ").

The idea of "more or less *like* a so-and-so" is quite eligible without any implications of "abnormal or imperfect" and seems necessary to any classifying procedure; it designates resemblance and degree of resemblance merely. And if cases to which a case in dispute is referred are said to be "standard" cases, the sense of 'standard' need not support ideas of decline from, or achievement of, some "standard" (that is, some model of excellence) but rather may allow responsibly for the extension of a classifying term to items that bear a resemblance to the "standard" (that is, the indisputable, the familiar). Here I think of a remark of Wittgenstein's: "Hence the importance of finding and inventing *intermediate cases*." [8] One may also notice that the expression 'paradigm case' may serve for both of these senses of 'standard.'

The argument may be turned around. We speak of something's being "more or less a so-and-so" in an evaluative way. For instance, "X is less of a man (or more of a man) than Y." Now, it is possible to say that when we evaluate something as good in a certain respect, we are in effect classifying it. This way of speaking may be allowable. But it has nothing whatever to do with the thesis that classifying itself entails "the idea of 'more or less a so-and-so.'" To put the matter broadly: evaluating may be taken to be classifying but classifying need not be evaluating.

Concede that some classifications allow directly for the idea of a good so-and-so. For instance, if I understand the use of the term 'knife' I will also understand the idea of a good knife. There must be an important difference then between such classifying terms as 'knife' and such terms as 'tiger' and 'man.' Still, the answer is obscured by the fact that, in some contexts, there may be a use for such phrases as 'good as a tiger' and 'good as a man.' Hampshire tries to accommodate our puzzlement here by noting:

> When the grounds of classification do not in any way involve the more or less constant part that the things classified play in human life, the phrase 'a good so-and-so' will not have a clear and constant sense. A determinate sense for the phrase will only be suggested by a particular context of use.

The difference between the two sorts of terms mentioned may now be made clear. The grounds for classifying things as knives will "involve the more or less constant part that the things classified play in human life"—that is, in terms of function or role or office or specialized relationship and the like; it will be possible to speak directly (in terms of the classifying procedure itself) of more or less good knives. But the classification of things as tigers or men does not show this same pattern; hence we cannot speak directly (in a *classificatory* sense merely) of more or less good tigers or more or less good men.

If this be admitted, then Hampshire must find himself in a dilemma. Because if 'tiger' and 'man' *may* be used in such a way that one may not yet be provided with a sense for 'good tiger' or 'good as a man,' Hampshire must concede his original thesis to be defeated; and if he insists that in "a particular context of use" some "determinate sense" may be given to such phrases, the particular context will in effect always *propose* a change in the classifying term itself to provide *now* for evaluation—which will defeat his original thesis.

The fact is that familiar classifying concepts may conceivably be used without any provision for "abnormal or imperfect" cases. This is not to say that such cases cannot be provided for. But the interesting thing is that provision for the idea of "more or less a so-and-so," for these concepts, will be taken to signify either that classifying and evaluating are distinct (that, say, only creatures *classified as men* can be more or less perfect or defective in those regards *in which* men can be more or less perfect or defective—the implication here being that one cannot be more or less perfect or defective merely in being a man) or that a *proposal* has been made to alter the sense of the original classificatory term so that it is now implicitly evaluative as well (hence the view that classifying necessarily provides for evaluation).

The question at stake is in reality the old question of the Platonic Dialogues. Hampshire himself understands it as such. But we have now an important clue to the sort of puzzled dissatisfaction that the analogy between a good knife and a good man generates. The very ground for classifying things as knives provides for the idea of "more or less good as a knife." Whatever new proposals we make about evaluating knives, we cannot escape the fact that in the very notion of a knife, classifying and evaluating are logically bound together. But though we may propose to use a term like 'man' in such a way that classifying and evaluating are again logically bound together, we cannot escape noticing that there always remains an independent classifying sense of 'man' that is free of evaluative implications —*a fortiori*, of moral implications.

What we are dissatisfied with in the Platonic argument is the claim that the concept 'man' *necessarily behaves in the same logical way as that of 'knife,'* that in *any* elucidation of the concept 'man' we will find implicit the notion of "more or less good as a man." The fear may not be entirely well-founded, but arguments of the sort Hampshire advances inevitably suggest that man's *excellence* may simply be discovered by examining his nature. So that, even when immutable essences are denied, one wonders how one is to read the claim that "there is no possibility that a man's family relationships, his knowledge and mental skills . . . should be dismissed as altogether irrelevant to his goodness or badness as a human being." The best we can do is to express human excellences in terms of human nature; we cannot determine them independently by consulting human nature. To put the matter perhaps too trimly: we may assign man his nature on the basis of his excellence, but from the nature of a knife we may derive its excellence.

Similarly and on even more general linguistic grounds, Zeno Vendler asks "What is a good man? What is man's function?" [9] He assures us that

> The conclusion forces itself upon us: to be a man, to be a person, is like having a function. In our original terminology: the co-occurrences *good-man* or *good-person* must determine an appropriate verb class; that is to say, there must be a set of activities with respect to which somebody can be qualified as good, not as a dancer, poet, or father, but simply as a man.

He links his linguistic findings to Aristotle's analogy between the function of a flute-player and the function of a man and also to Paul Ziff's "surmise that the principles determining the rank of an adjective have something to do with natural kinds." But the argument is indecisive, affecting both the prospects of metaethics and the power of linguistic methods to resolve philosophical questions of quite different sorts.

Vendler holds, correctly, that "things that have no natural use can be put to some use or other, and objects with a natural use still can be put to other uses or misuses"—though this is not a linguistic insight, however consistent it may be with the distinctive provisions of a language. He himself says of the following list of sentences:

John is a good dancer.
John is a good poet.
John is a good father.
John is a good man.
Fido is a good dog.
Mumbo is a good baboon.

"In the sad case of Mumbo, the good baboon, we are entirely at a loss; being a baboon is certainly not having a function; moreover, baboons ordinarily are not things that acquire functions, either. What is it that a good baboon is supposed to do well?"—which is surely an extra-linguistic insight. Vendler thinks, however, that "some intelligibility remains with *good dog*" because "after all there are some basic requirements that *all* good dogs (sheep dogs, hunting dogs, and so on) must meet: faithfulness, obedience, and the like, which, as it were, form *the common denominator* in regard to these functions." And it is apparently in the spirit of these remarks that he comes to the conclusion that "somebody can be qualified as good, not as a dancer, poet, or father, but simply as a man."

I wish to emphasize first of all that whether there is an alleged common denominator for all dogs is not a question that can be resolved on grammatical grounds at all. Precisely because dogs do not have a natural function (Vendler is prepared to say that "it is nonsense to say that Fido is good as a dog"), one could not show that the various species of dogs share excellences common to the genus. Put in another way, there is no doubt that, with respect to classification in terms of the function of sheep dogs, hunting dogs, and the like, specimen animals are not examined under the genus dog at all (though such classification may well have been presupposed); or, again, *sheep dog*, *hunting dog* are themselves indissoluble classificatory terms whose use does entail reference to some proper function. The same, I should hold, is true of the relationship among the terms *man, postman, porter, sailor, father, candlestickmaker*—which shows how misleading the particle *-man* may actually be. On linguistic grounds, again, I should draw attention to the important difference between saying that Fido is good as a dog and saying that Fido is good as a hunting dog. (Notice also the possible force of saying that John is good as a postman— which may suggest that something else is lacking; he is per- haps, though of course not necessarily, not good as a father, or he is perhaps not a good man). We characteristically drop the form 'as a . . .' for all phrases in which the classificatory term does not involve a natural or proper function (though I shall return to this point). Clearly, 'as a . . .' has what may be called an *aspective* use, that is, a use in which a kind of thing is viewed in a restricted respect. Dogs, considered as hunting dogs, may be good in the way hunting dogs are good; but dogs, merely as dogs, cannot be said to be good (in a similar sense).

Secondly, there is no clear way to determine whether there are and what are the "basic requirements that all good dogs . . . must meet." I should not deny that, characteristically, in saying that Fido is a good dog, I should be referring in some sense to distinctly doggish qualities—though even this is not necessary (reference may be intended to his health, which may have more to do with his being canine, or a mammal, or even an animal). But suppose I meant that Fido is a distinctly lively dog, would I, declaring that Fido is a good dog, be committing an error of some sort, linguistic or metaphysical? In saying that Fido is a good dog, I need not be saying anything whatsoever related to the function, or to an alleged function, or even to an assigned function, of dogs; and whether the use of 'as a . . .' signifies or does not signify a natural or proper function is, quite simply, grammatically indeterminate. I cannot see that 'good' cannot function merely to express a very general pro- attitude toward a dog (admittedly for reasons that are not given), on the condition that there is no natural or proper function of dogs or basic requirements which are common to all good dogs. In general, there are no merely linguistic grounds which show that the quadruple uses (on Vendler's account) of an adjective like 'good' are related to one another in such a way that *if* phrases like 'good man,' 'good dog' are "understandable," there must be a function or something like a function assignable to men and dogs. There is no syntactical evidence at all that could determine this, and the semantical evidence is inherently indecisive (hence the vigor of the philosophical dispute).

I said before that we characteristically drop the aspective phrase 'as a . . .' for things that lack a natural or proper function. But I should also say that retaining the phrase does not entail that there is such a function assignable. Vendler takes it that since John may be good not as a poet but as a man, "the conclusion *forces itself* upon us," that to be a man is to have a function. But this simply begs the question (the question, for instance, facing Plato's and Aristotle's moral philosophies) of whether the excellences *assigned* to men answer to their natural or proper function. The phrase 'as a man' merely draws attention to the fact that we do judge men *qua* men (uniquely, it seems; or, by extension perhaps, along with gods and the like). But it forces us to conclude neither that, in doing so, we are judging them in terms of their function nor that, in judging them, we are agreed about the basic requirements or common denominator of all good men. What we see here is the inability of purely linguistic considerations to decide the conceptual issues of moral philosophy on the strength of the admissibility of phrases like 'as a. . . .' Any convention regarding normative values will support the linguistic pattern in question.

In short the grammar of 'good' (as of 'right' and 'ought' and the like is (and is demonstrably) completely unilluminating regarding the overriding values proper to human nature.

PART TWO

CHAPTER 6

Cognitivism and Moral Institutions

APART FROM MERE INERTIA, the conservation of our moral categories appears most promisingly open to defense by way of cognitivist claims and the implications of holding to certain critical portions of our descriptive vocabulary. For, if we can be said to know what is right or wrong or the like, in a sense stronger than that of merely recognizing conventional distinctions, moral skepticism and would-be moral reform may be challenged and tested in perfectly straightforward ways; and if the proper use of certain descriptive predicates—for instance, those that involve ascribing certain roles, functions, relationships, as of being a father, a policeman, a lifeguard, a promisor, a debtor—entails an entire system of norms and rules, then, perhaps, merely to use such predicates is to subscribe to the implied norms.[1] The trouble is that the claims of moral cognitivism are absurdly weak and the implied norms are obviously open to radical reform and even abolition. Under such circumstances, we may well wonder about the conceptual stability of the moral domain itself.

Now, moral cognitivism tends to take two quite different forms; most of the relevant theories of our own century have been either naturalistic or intuitionistic. But these are not merely competing theories; they are theories of quite different sorts. The naturalist claims that the meaning of critical predicates like 'good,' 'right,' 'ought,' and the like can be given in terms of so-called "natural" qualities, that is, qualities that can them-selves be discriminated by antecedently admitted cognitive fac-ulties—such as our capacity to discriminate pleasure, desire, its satisfaction, and the like[2]—faculties not themselves directed to the discrimination of normative elements as such. Questions naturally arise here regarding the conceptual connection be-tween descriptive and normative predicates; but these do not, as we have seen, adversely affect the tenability of naturalism. Intuitionist claims, on the other hand, are claims about a distinct faculty of moral perception or cognition, by which we are enabled to examine conduct and character and uniquely dis-criminate the presence of irreducibly moral qualities.[3]

The trouble with naturalism is that it is quite impossible to identify in a suitably neutral way the initial, the putatively moral data that this theory is supposed to be an induction from or an explanation of. Alternatively put, every naturalistic pro-posal—seemingly formulated at the metaethical level—is bound merely to reflect and codify those substantive ethical convictions that are otherwise subject to challenge and dispute by partisans of alternative values. If, for instance, he were to hold that 'good' means 'pleasant,' and 'right' means 'instrumental to producing good,' a naturalist would be bound, on pain of defeating his own thesis, to deny, as an admissible moral datum, the judgment (of however convinced an antagonist) that an act may sometimes be judged to be right without regard to ulterior good or even in the face of reducing or excluding good (a judgment which may be accompanied by the other's appropriate metaethical theory). But this means that substantive ethical disputes are only seem-ingly raised to some neutral level in turning to debate the tenability of naturalism itself. In the face of ethical disagree-ments of the relevant sort, it is quite dubious that an operative distinction can be made between ethical and metaethical issues: to subscribe to a particular naturalistic claim is effectively to de-cide substantive ethical issues; and to quarrel relevantly about these is to challenge the correctness and even the independence of such a claim. There is no non-question-begging way by which to identify the primary data to be accommodated, except by identifying what is conventionally or sincerely taken by particular persons to be a moral issue and a correct moral judgment; but to proceed thus is to proceed with less than one might otherwise require and, of course, to countenance all substantive quarrels imaginable. It is precisely because moral values are overriding values, that the selection of paradigm judgments and behavior is inevitably decisive in assessing competing theories: moral partisans cannot admit all their opponents' views as full-fledged specimens about which *they* are to theorize.

The intuitionist, on the other hand, cannot foreclose, except by fiat, any of the disputes of the sort that confront naturalists, for ethical disagreement is a fundamental datum of the domain if any is. Also, the intuitionist's claim is even more obviously *ad hoc* than that of his naturalistic counterpart. He will never be able to explain to those presumably not suitably gifted, or not aware of their gift, what non-moral features may serve as criteria for learning to make correct moral judgments;[4] and he will never be able to provide public criteria for adjudicating disputes between alleged intuitions that happen to collide.[5] If he were to offer such criteria, he would obviate the need for intuitionism itself; and if he did not, he would be forced to settle disputes by pronouncement only. Then too, there is no remotely plausible theory of the nature of the required gift of moral intuition—corresponding, for example, to the kind of theory that may be provided for the senses of sight and hearing. The required intuition cannot be fundamental to the domain, for its exercise is obviously private; and it cannot be a dependent or subsidiary faculty like that of telepathy or clairvoyance, for there is no other fundamental faculty by which to test its power.

All in all, these considerations undermine the prospects of cognitivism, by showing that the grounds on which it is ordinarily defended are inherently question-begging or arbitrary. To say this, however, is not to say that, given moral norms, rules, criteria, one cannot judge or know what is right or wrong or the like. It is only to say that the relevant sorts of judgment presuppose such a system (which may vary from society to society and, within societies, from group to group or from period to period, and may always be contested on the strength of alternative principles and convictions). Cognitivism, if it were to succeed, would have to be able to provide for a convincing distinction between real and apparent values, not only within given systems (which is the normal purpose of any particular partisan doctrine) but also between incompatible and competing systems (which leads us back to the difficulties already put forward).

No theory supporting the cognitive role of perception, it may be observed, can fail to provide for systematic and public distinctions between real and apparent perception—for all relevant claims; but it is hard to see how a corresponding theory can be constructed, along intuitionist lines, for the supposed faculty of moral sentience. In the perceptual analogue, considerations respecting the publicity of perceptual confirmation and the coherence of particular claims with the entire body of our knowledge are paramount. In the moral domain, on the contrary, the appeal to intuition appears to be little more than an emphatic insistence on preferred values and judgment; the public convergence of values may be a pious hope, but it is not the result of a clear application of public procedures of inquiry. There is also, as we have seen, no theory of normative human nature (corresponding to our theory of mere physical nature) that facilitates predictive and corrective moves respecting particular claims; such apparent theories are tantamount merely to sketches of those very claims themselves and are not even primarily designed to service or fit causal inquiries. There simply are no conceptually convincing grounds for speaking of the discovery of normative human values.

One may put all of this, schematically, in historical terms, holding that Moore, in his famous discussion of the so-called

Naturalistic Fallacy, managed to show that *if* 'good' designates a quality different from any other particular quality, then it would be a mistake to take the two as the same quality.[6] But the truth is a trivial and irrelevant one; for what we wish to know—what Moore thought he was pressing—is the answer to the question whether *good* is the same as any named quality, such as "being the object of an interest" or "pleasant" or the like. The slightest reflection shows that we are not in the least clear how to demonstrate that 'good' does or does not mean this or that. The reason is elementary; for if people, on the basis of their lives and linguistic practice, sincerely subscribe to different *criteria* of what is good, we shall have to be careful, in attempting to answer Moore's question, to avoid construing the *meaning* of 'good' in such a way as to prejudice the assessment of competing criteria or competing values. But the only way in which to do this is to provide an answer that is either not responsive to Moore's question or else to recover a genuinely viable cognitivism. With respect to the first alternative, one might for instance have defined 'good' as 'possessing merit,' but this is obviously trivial and raises precisely the same question; or one might have said that 'good' means 'answering to certain interests'[7] (which, as it stands, is not responsive, in the sense that it does not accommodate the distinctively normative feature of moral judgments or provide for the specification of criteria relative to that feature). The second alternative we have already found to be more than doubtful, inasmuch as there are no clear or even barely uncontroversial ways to proceed to an answer. Cognitivism, then, is an unsupportable thesis, though to say this is not to deny that particular moral judgments can be true or false, known to be so, and defensible by the provision of supporting evidence.

To turn to the question of the moral import of certain descriptive predicates, it is quite clear that these concern the internal institutions of particular societies. To infer (correctly) the obligations of office that bind a man functioning as a lifeguard is simply to grasp the nature of that institutionalized role in our society. I may, however, emphasize here that one may be tempted, quite mistakenly, to recover by way of an apparently linguistic theory all that is jeopardized by the indefensibility of cognitivism. But it is possible, without any linguistic dislocation, both to alter the duties of lifeguards consistently with their proper function and to alter or abolish the role altogether. If one thinks of kings and rulers, husbands and fathers, friends and neighbors, it is clear that neither internal reform nor external variations can be convincingly resisted by an appeal to the merely conventional moral implications of the use of the relevant descriptive predicates. What, for instance, is the function of a ruler (*pace* Socrates) or a neighbor, that could in any detailed way guide judgment and conduct.[8] Terms of this sort occupy an interesting limbo in the sense that they designate offices, functions, institutionalized relationships, with respect to which their *sense* (by contrast with that of 'postman,' 'knife,' and the like) does not entail any relevant.*criteria* of a normative sort. The reason, as we may guess, is that terms like 'ruler' and 'neighbor' and 'friend' are more clearly relevant to disputes about alternative ideals of life than are the others. We shall return to the issue below.

Still, moral criticism, moral reform, moral theories of every stripe must begin with the recognition of the characteristic distinctions of conventional morality. For, whatever moral innovation one has to offer, one can only suppose that, in advancing a particular doctrine, he is advancing a doctrine like *that,* like the one that obtains for the society at large (however much under criticism and doubt). Here, it may be misleading to mark out the boundaries of the domain of the *moral*; any proposed distinction threatens to preclude the admission of would-be theories that might otherwise challenge the adoption of other prominent contenders. Moral theories are theories concerning the justification of human conduct, in normative and overriding terms: but this gives only a sense of the unity of the domain, not positive criteria by which to admit or deny the admissibility or force of particular theories. If we take the categorical term 'moral' to have normative import itself, it will be as much a counter for competing theories as the appraisive terms actually used in moral judgment; and if we take it to provide no more than a rough-and-ready demarcation of a domain of inquiry, it will be less than helpful to dispute its definition. Correspondingly, one cannot usefully ask why one ought to be moral,[9] unless to have its sense explained along the lines already provided. For, either an indefinitely varied and contingent answer may be given, in the sense that morality may prove to be instrumental to some ulterior values held by this or that agent (financial, prudential, religious, etc.); or any allegedly conceptual connection between putative moral values and ulterior values—such that the latter must be admitted to take precedence over the former—will oblige us merely to construe the ulterior values as themselves the true, overriding values. In the latter instance, the original question will apply properly; otherwise, the question will dwindle on in a useless regress.

Also, the thesis that morality is ultimately justified on prudential grounds is a muddled one. For, if one takes prudential values to be *overriding values for a rational agent,* there will then be no possible distinction between moral and prudential issues: by this view, trivially, whatever values are justified on moral (or prudential) grounds will, *ipso facto,* be prudential (or moral) as well. This appears, equivocally, for example, in the views of Thrasymachus and Karl Marx. As soon as rationality is construed as setting limits of an overriding sort on whatever conduct an agent may prefer, there is no point in distinguishing morality from prudence. Prudence must, as a distinct concern, be restricted to instrumental considerations or to instrumental considerations within the framework of what I can only call presumptive interests. For example, it may be a presumptive interest of a prudential man to preserve his life and to avoid pain, but it cannot, on conceptual grounds alone, be contrary to *rational* conduct as such, to commit suicide or to sacrifice one's life or to pursue masochistic pleasures or to accept a significant amount of pain in the pursuit of one's interests. Spinoza's insistence on the irrationality of suicide, for instance, predictably collapses the moral and the prudential by assigning man conative drives of a normative and overriding sort. Alternatively put, the formula that "it is by definition necessary that every rational being should seek his own interests as far as possible" [10] is incapable of justifying the construction of any particular presumptive interests as interests *necessary* to rationality itself—without assuming, further, a knowledge of normative human nature. The presumptive interests of a (prudent) man may be set aside in the name of higher presumptive interests (as when a man accepts a considerable amount of pain as the price of surgery that may save his life); and they may be set aside in the name of higher non-prudential interests (as when a man sacrifices his life for a cause he thinks is a worthy one). Presumptive interests are merely those that do not call for specific justification in order to count as rational and intelligible; they are neither overriding nor necessary interests for rational agents. Even a would-be suicide may be a rational suicide, though he act contrary to obvious presumptive interests. Prudence and morality differ, then, in that the one is concerned with contingent and presumptive values and the other, with overriding values. Consequently, either the formula given above is false since moral objectives may be rationally pursued contrary to the prudential interests of an agent, or it is vacuous since an agent may rationally pursue what he claims as his "interest" even contrary to admittedly presumptive interests.

The denial of cognitivism, therefore, appears to have radical implications, for one wonders about the possibility of providing justifying grounds for moral innovation and reform as well as for conserving the system one inherits. The problem is easily misconstrued as requiring an emotivist answer—which is, in a sense, the counterpart to skepticism with respect to perceptual claims.[11] The inherent limitation of emotivism is just that it makes no provision whatsoever for the justification of ethical claims. Emotivism is simply false relative to any given ethical system: both findings and appreciative judgments, as we have seen, are debated and assessed (in logically distinct ways) within the institutionalized life of every familiar society. What, however, needs to be clarified is the logical status of alternative sorts of criticism and reform of, and reasoned departure from, *existing* ethical institutions; for it is in the context of such considerations (if anywhere) that emotivism may claim a foothold.

Consider, in this connection, one of Jesus' ethical reforms:

> Ye have heard that it was said by them of old time,
> Thou shalt not commit adultery:
> But I say unto you, That whosoever looketh on a
> woman to lust after her hath committed adultery
> with her already in heart.[12]

The reform is intended, clearly, for at least those subscribing to the commandment, Thou shalt not commit adultery. (It is also, doubtless, intended for all men, but that is another matter.) The argument appears to be that, given that the overt act of adultery is forbidden, other *acts* ("whosoever looketh on a woman to lust after her") involving the same illicit motives and attitudes already proscribed may reasonably be covered by an extension of the morally significant term 'adultery.' Or, consider the enhanced arguability of a Marxist reform of private property—given the institution of private property—if the labor theory of value were confirmed. Arguments of these sorts, concerning *reform*, may be construed as conditional arguments.

The signal feature of these intended reforms is this: that, although the underlying concern is obviously a moral one, the reasonableness of the extensions and changes advocated is debatable, and debatable on grounds quite analogous to those supporting the systematic adjustment of all descriptive and classificatory terms, whether value-laden or not and whether morally relevant or not. Imagine, for instance, that geese and ducks are initially distinguished solely on the basis of perceivable anatomical and gross physiological differences; on this basis, the so-called Andean goose, which, as Konrad Lorenz claims, "lives like a goose, looks like a goose, and grazes like a goose," will continue to be called a goose. Perhaps behavioral as well as genetic considerations (apparently, it exhibits the sheldrake's courtship behavior) will incline us to extend the term 'duck' to such a creature and, at the same time, to *alter* the criteria on which, for systematically advantageous reasons, geese and ducks and other creatures are henceforth to be distinguished: our Andean goose will then be "nothing but a sheldrake that has evolved along the lines of a goose." What needs to be seen here is that a genuine reform (whether with respect to the classification of fauna or with respect to the moral criticism of conduct) is open to appraisal along lines that essentially concern the systematic adjustment of the details of a theory designed to accommodate an entire, fairly-well demarcated domain. In the instance of biological classification, considerations of causal explanation will be paramount and decisive; classification will be corrected in the sense of being made to conform with evolutionary and genetic theory. In the instance of moral evaluation, the coherence and scope of covering principles appear to be most decisive (there being, it must be conceded, no single system to which we must converge).

Here, then, is the key to the deepest conceptual puzzles respecting the justification of sustaining or reforming any given system of conventional morality. The defense of the categories of moral discrimination and judgment do not depend, as do counterpart distinctions in the sciences, on systematic causal considerations. Furthermore, there are no cognitive faculties, in the moral domain, corresponding to the faculty of perception, on which (without ignoring complications due to the theory-laden nature of perceptual claims and reports) an initial body of data may be posited, *that is relatively independent* of the metamoral theories to be tested. Also, moral theorists are inevitably moral partisans; so that the coherence of any given theory must, to some extent, be relativized to the moral convictions of particular agents. Nevertheless, precisely because the details of every conventional morality can be known and described and because every departure from, or reform of, institutionalized moral practice and judgment must depend on a systematic reference to such practice and judgment, there is a fair sense in which the ultimate justificatory principles of any given metamoral theory may be assessed in terms of their coherence and scope—without, be it noted, supposing that alternative and even incompatible theories cannot be reasonably defended. (We shall return to this issue at a later point.) The upshot is that metamoral theories cannot, when properly defended, be construed as true but only as plausible.[13] Emotivism will still be untenable, then, for it will have failed to gain its point even in the most favorable circumstance, namely, where one moral code is being replaced by another. If we allow that alternative reforms may be proposed along competing lines of extension, it may well be that the preference of one or another (as well as of a conservative resistance to change) may depend on an appreciative bias or conviction; this, however, is not to say that justificatory reasons cannot be given for a proposed extension or change (which may be appraised in ways that are relatively similar for all classificatory adjustments—hence, in ways that are not, as such, morally freighted) but only that, contingent on the governing preference, the logic of the relevant reasoning is of a weaker sort (being concerned with plausibility) than is available elsewhere.

Moral reform, like classificatory reform, presupposes an existing system which, for reasons noticeably relevant to the domain to be codified but not yet provided for in the system governing the domain, ought (so it is claimed) to be reformed; we are speaking, of course, of conceptual reforms, not those concerned with social engineering. This clearly distinguishes reform from possibly radical departures from conventional moral thinking, that may be found in the abrupt adoption of some extreme ideal or way of life. The rational egoist, for instance, seizing the implications of his principle, may reject all conventional distinctions respecting duty, rights, obligations, and the like. Similarly, a Western man who adopts some severe version of contemplative Buddhism may—without denying the relevance of distinctions covered by 'right,' 'ought,' 'duty,' 'justice,' and the like—reject particular responsibilities and pursuits otherwise thought to be binding or worthwhile in a Western code of conduct and may prefer altogether alien duties. Here, although the specimen reforms and departures indicated both depend on appreciative judgments, the justifying considerations *relevant to the changes or departures proposed* are of strikingly different sorts. Emotivism will remain untenable, but disputes about reform will prove to be inherently more systematic and constraining than disputes about alternative ideals of life.

The reason is simply that the logic of reform concerns debate over changes in a system that, at least provisionally, allows for findings and the confirmation of findings; the proposed changes admittedly depend upon appreciative preferences, possibly even of a global sort since they may involve considerable revision in the theoretical defense of the institutions at stake. But apart from these preferences, which, after all, are responsible for positing particular proposals to be pursued, the reasonableness of reforms advocated may be assessed in terms of the comparative coherence, scope, arbitrariness, and the like of the altered categories; and this is both sufficient to upset emotivism and the best that we can expect. If, for instance, overt adultery is condemned because the overt act is, among other things, committed with a lustful intent, then (considerations of detection and control aside) acts substantially short of overt adultery but significantly informed by the very same or similar lustful intent call for a relevant decision on the propriety of a corresponding condemnation; the extension of 'adultery' registers this analogy (which happens to be morally significant) and the argument for or against extension will be at least minimally constrained by noticeable similarities and differences (the detection of which does not depend on partisan moral convictions). Similarly, the development of an ethical code governing international relations must evolve by extrapolating values from the ethically relevant but restricted practices of the affected communities. Alternative arguments will, to be sure, seek to alter the extension of critical predicates along different lines (think, for example, of international relations in outer space or merely of the adversary system in the law); and rational decision, however it may depend on an appreciative preference for one or another of the theoretical accounts, will be bound to confine its verdict within a range of at least minimally plausible alternatives. To construe this as somehow confirming emotivism is, quite obviously, to read emotivism merely as a cognitivism *manqué*. Sometimes, as in the legal tradition, the prospect and need of regular, if piecemeal, reform is so clearly recognized that procedures internal to the system actually provide for reform (that is, without predetermining the content of substantive changes—which would preclude reform as such); and there, we find ourselves on the borderline between findings and appreciative judgments, for the transition is affected by an institutionalized reliance on the practice of rendering, appealing, and accepting authoritative verdicts. A community thereby restricts its reliance on the vagaries of appreciative preference and, by a process that combines decision and appraisal, establishes a halfway house that appears to extend the competence of findings and to reduce the possible arbitrariness of appreciative judgment. In any case, given the relative informality of definitions and criteria in the moral domain, as well as the subtle evolution of complex institutions, gradual extensions of critical predicates—even where reform is not explicit—are inescapable and provide paradigms for deliberate and reasoned change. On the other hand, departures from established morality that occur because someone or some group has decided to subscribe to novel ideals (for instance, vegetarianism, Buddhist asceticism, hippiedom, or the like) are departures primarily respecting what is inherently a matter of appreciative preference. No question arises here about the reform of provisionally acceptable ranges of findings, although that the ideals in question may require a reinterpretation of portions of conventional, institutionalized morality is hardly surprising. The question will occupy us again.

These considerations profoundly affect the strategy of moral debate. The matter may be conveniently focussed by attending to the distinction between alleged duties to self and to others (of whatever sort these duties may be taken to be); for duties of these two kinds cannot be treated, in all relevant respects, in parallel ways. Duties to self cannot be defended at all, except on the basis of some theory of normative human nature or of some human ideal; and since, as we have already seen, there are no defensible grounds on which claims about normative human nature may be cognitively grounded, judgments of such alleged duties cannot be logically stronger than appreciative judgments. On the other hand, duties to others arise, at least provisionally, on the basis of certain functions, roles, relationships involving others, within the context of the institutional life of a society —sometimes entered into voluntarily (as in promising and making contracts), sometimes merely entailed by one's participation in the life of the society (as in becoming a parent or functioning as a citizen). If a man may be said to enter into the relevant relationships with himself (as, perhaps, in contracting with himself in two distinct roles), then, *per accidens,* he may have such duties or obligations to himself; but these are not what we understand by duties to self as such. Kant's specimen instances, for example—the alleged duty not to take one's own life and the duty to develop one's own talents—are assignable, presumably, to persons on the strength of no other consideration than that of being a person; the question of established relationships to others is beside the point. To deny, however, that an inspection (of whatever sort) of human nature may provide a basis for deriving duties to self is not to deny that telling reasons may be advanced for insisting on such duties—only that they cannot be taken to support a finding. By way of contrast, judgments about duties to others, at least provisionally for the institutionalized life of a society, may be, and are, construed as findings. A cognitivism of some sort would be required to convert judgments regarding duties to self into findings; but, given the context of institutionalized life, the construction of judgments of duties to others need not presuppose any form of cognitivism at all. Whether, for instance, a rationally pursued sadism is a morally desirable life for a human being depends on appreciative preferences regarding human potentialities; but whether taking another's life is morally defensible depends, at least provisionally, on the institutionalized norms of a particular society. Also, therefore, alleged duties to others advanced on the basis of presumptive interests or overriding values for human nature—again, in the manner of Kant's discussion of the duty to contribute to the happiness of others—depends on appreciative preferences. But to say this is to admit the incompleteness of the account, both with respect to ulterior grounds for defending particular societal institutions and with respect to the relationship between the defense of institutions and the defense of human ideals; for we have already admitted that duties associated with particular offices, roles, and relationships may be altered and particular institutions abolished, and we cannot deny that a comprehensive moral theory should examine the joint coherence of what is expected, normatively, of men with regard to one another and with regard to themselves.

CHAPTER 7

Institutions and the Identification of Acts

THERE IS A NEST OF STRATEGIES by which to avoid the uncomfortable conclusion that moral norms are a matter of social convention. We have found a number of these strategies deficient. For instance, we have found it impossible to defend the view that man has a normative nature open in any sense to discovery. We have also found moral cognitivism to be utterly untenable; and we have found that there is no merit in the seemingly linguistic thesis that the (linguistically) correct use of relevant expressions entails a commitment to corresponding moral norms. The pervasiveness of the latter strategy is hardly appreciated; in fact, the ubiquity of moral distinctions embedded in the most familiar discourse blinds us to the theoretical possibility of quite radically altering our descriptions of human behavior. One comes to believe, then, that the categories of moral assessment are of such fixity that relevant judgments of human conduct must be construed as findings of a theoretically firmer sort than may be provided by merely adhering to persistent and widespread custom. The question quite naturally arises, therefore, as to the nature of our description and explanation of human acts and actions—with particular attention to the moral context. We are bound to go somewhat far afield, in order to provide a sense of closure respecting the strategies noted, to clarify some of the general features of our discourse about human action. We shall find, by our detour, confirmation of the deep sense in which the description of human action—seemingly not at all restricted to moral questions—reflects the institutions, norms, and conventions of a society, and we shall also find the sense in which the usual justification of actions committed (or contemplated) depends in a distinctive and important way on the assumption of relevant social norms. The consequence is that one cannot gain an independent purchase on normative moral values by considering the nature of the description and explanation of human action. But if this maneuver is blocked, it would appear to be quite impossible to deny that moral norms are essentially conventions embedded in the institutionalized life of a society—subject, therefore, to reform or alteration or even rejection on the strength of systematic convictions regarding the overriding values of human life. Correspondingly, maneuvers of the sort in question may be fairly labeled "crypto-cognitivism."[1]

To turn to our issue, the ascription of morally relevant predicates and the identification of genuine acts and actions are not deployed along congruent, but rather intersecting, lines of use. The concept of human action, in fact, serves a double duty, bridging in an interesting way the explanation of physical phenomena and the evaluation of the details of human life. Questions arise, on the one hand, about the reduction of human actions to physical events, about the relationship between causal explanations and explanations by way of reasons, motives, intentions, purposes, and the like and, on the other, about the analysis of human responsibility and freedom and about the grounds for the criteria by which human behavior is assessed. The implication is that one must be extremely circumspect, in speaking of the conceptual role of acts and actions in the moral domain, of theorizing about the nature of human action itself.

It has been suggested that, as a general rule, "an action is called an act only when it can be described in a proposition with a personal subject; the actions of signing a check or killing a rival are acts, for one can say, 'I signed the check,' or 'He killed his rival'; but the beating of the heart and the working of the liver are not acts. . . ." An alternative version of the rule is that "one may substitute 'act' for 'action' only when the action may be spoken of as 'my action'. . . ." [2] But this is not entirely satisfactory. For one thing, the rule is conditional on the antecedent identification of bona fide actions: 'I bled' and 'my bleeding' meet the tests but they sort out no actions.[3] And, for another, the satisfaction of the test may be due merely to accidents of language; we might, for instance, possess a verb 'to coronate,' meaning 'to beat, as in particular in the heart's beating'; in that case, we might possess the expressions 'I coronated' and 'my coronating'—which would complicate our sorting out acts and actions from what merely happens to us.

Acts and actions form a certain collection of the things termed events (or occurrences, happenings, episodes, and the like). We may, in fact, order an informal series of related collections of apparently decreasing extension that bear on questions of human responsibility and behavior as follows: events, deeds, actions, acts. In this series, 'deeds' is a relatively technical term; it is quite often used as a synonym for 'acts,' but I shall use it as the substantive answering to the verb 'do' (in grammatically suitable tenses), where the subject is a personal agent. It seems reasonable to hold, inasmuch as deeds include not only acts and actions but also such happenings as one's bleeding, that the considerations on which things are sorted out as deeds and actions are, to some extent, not quite systematically related to one another. I suggest that wherever happenings (like coughing, bleeding, dying, sleeping) are of sufficient importance to *persons* —for instance, by being closely linked to the presumptive interests of prudential agents—the relevant use of the personal pronoun is characteristically employed: hence the indecisiveness of the absence of a verb like 'coronate.'

Now, it is helpful to observe that, although events are identified as deeds if they are of sufficient importance to persons (so that, for instance, they bear on the range of goals that ordinarily occupy the efforts people make, that count as acts and actions), questions of moral responsibility and of moral evaluation do not arise *simpliciter* for deeds as such. My dying, for instance, may causally affect the adequacy of providing for my children; but whether I am to blame, posthumously, for inadequate provision occasioned by my dying can only be decided by locating the deed additionally in a suitable context of responsibility and moral appraisal. My deeds (other than my acts and actions) *may* justify judgments of responsibility, blame, excuse, and the like; but deeds as such appear to be entirely neutral as far as moral issues are concerned. The same is not true, significantly, for acts. For, if I have committed (or if I am thought to have committed) a murder, then at once moral judgments are at least relevant, even though a valid appraisal would require a proper study of the circumstances in which the act occurred or is alleged to have occurred; on the other hand, if I have performed the act of turning on the ignition in my automobile, it is not the case that moral judgment is at once construed as relevant. Some acts and actions, when merely identified, are identified as such in morally relevant ways; others are not but may, rather as with deeds, be placed in a suitable context of moral responsibility and evaluation. My turning on the ignition, in the context of suicide, becomes morally significant in much the same way as my dying, in the context of a dissolute life. But terms descriptive of acts and actions fall into distinct groupings, some being morally and not morally significant, some valuationally and not valuationally significant. The difference repays study.

We may make a fresh start by considering acts in the context of a game of chess. The act of pushing a black, distinctly shaped object across a board may be described as such without regard to the rules of chess or, in fact, without regard to any rules at all; but the act of putting the king in check cannot be identified as such without reference to the constitutive rules of chess. Furthermore, within the context of playing chess, the act cannot be ignored or redescribed in any way that obscures its occurrence. For example, the redescription of the act as mating the king, if true, is allowable, since mating the king may be accomplished by putting the king in check and since mating the king is the object of the game; but the redescription of the act as moving one's fifth piece into one's opponent's half of the board—though independently allowable and conceivably even relevant in a game of chess—obscures the occurrence of moves that are essential to the pursuit of the game. There is a point, in a game of chess, where the consequences of given acts cannot be admissibly elided with the acts themselves in a proper redescription of what has occurred and a point where alternative descriptions cannot replace the descriptions in question, are in fact relatively impertinent to the activity of chess play. It appears, therefore, that games like chess, strictly defined by rules of play, specify in effect a range of acts proper to the game itself. Limits of elision, both minimal and maximal, are imposed on all relevant descriptions of acts within the game: some acts are not yet acts within the game of chess and some are acts that pass beyond the context of the game; and, within the game, the elision of act and consequence is restricted by considerations of relevance to admissible and essential plays and the object of the game.

The trouble, returning to the moral context, is that life is not, in the requisite sense, a game. It is extremely difficult to maintain the thesis (and yet we are inclined to) that constraints on the description and redescription of human acts can, within the moral domain, be said to be governed by rules or rule-like considerations so as to set limits upon the elision of acts and consequences and upon the substitution of one description for another.

Let us examine in some detail, therefore, the central thesis of Eric D'Arcy's study of human acts—the most explicit and interesting version, perhaps, of the doctrine in question, to have appeared in recent print. D'Arcy holds that

> *Certain kinds of act are of such significance that the terms which denote them may not, special contexts apart, be elided*

into terms which (a) denote their consequences, and (b) conceal, or even fail to reveal, the nature of the act itself. Typical examples are the acts of killing, maiming, slandering, torturing, deceiving, or seriously offending another person; betraying or deserting a friend or an ally; breaking a contract or a promise or a confidence; stealing or destroying or spoiling something which the owner, or the community, looks on as precious; sacrificing or endangering one's own happiness, good name, health, or property. For instance, 'Macbeth stabbed Duncan and, as a consequence, killed him,' may be re-described simply as 'Macbeth killed Duncan'; but 'Macbeth killed Duncan and, as a consequence, succeeded him,' may not be re-described simply as, 'Macbeth succeeded Duncan.' To quote a more recent example, it was alleged during the Eichmann trial that a Nazi research institute asked a concentration-camp commandant to supply it with a number of infant bodies for use in some experiments, and that in order to comply with this request the commandant had the required number of babies of Jewish women prisoners gassed. Now to describe his act as 'assisting medical research,' or 'promoting the advancement of science,' simply would not do, even though research may have been assisted or scientific knowledge advanced as a result of his act. Taking human life, we feel, is an act of such significance that one cannot elide its description into a term which denotes its consequence, or an end to which it was a means, unless that term makes clear that this was the means used.[4]

There is, of course, the danger that D'Arcy's thesis may be interpreted as analytically true; that, insofar as acts are taken to be of the required "significance," the terms denoting them and their consequences may not be elided in the manner indicated (as in cases involving what "the owner, or the community, looks on as precious"). But D'Arcy appears to be holding rather that "certain kinds of acts *are*" of the significance required, whether or not particular persons think so—perhaps whether or not entire communities think so. He seems to be reminding us here of what he takes to be a truism and offers no evidence to support his claim. Nevertheless, the thesis is false—but important.

Consider, for instance, a society in which the incumbent king is—as *we* might say—the successful murderer of the previous king; that is, consider a society whose customs are such that title to the throne may be legitimately established by being causally responsible for the death of the current king. Such a society might very easily agree with the views on murder of our own society, with the single exception of this matter of monarchical succession. In *that* case, contrary to what D'Arcy says, the consequence of succeeding to the throne could, reasonably, be elided with the description of killing—our man could, under the circumstances, be said to have performed the act of establishing his legitimate title to the throne (there might even be other ways of gaining the throne, as by besting the incumbent in a formal match of hand-wrestling). The interesting and even deadly import of this is that the Nazi research instance that D'Arcy himself cites is, logically, of precisely the same sort. And this means that he cannot disqualify redescriptions of human acts that elide consequences and acts in a way that, *to our mind but not to theirs,* might obscure the dire significance of these acts for "human existence and welfare and happiness." He cannot, that is, without a substantially more pertinent argument.

We must be careful here. D'Arcy does admit that terms like 'murder,' 'mayhem,' and 'betrayal' have built into them "some sort of moral judgment"; but he thinks that some like 'kill,' 'maim,' and 'deceive' "may be purely factual and descriptive." His thesis, therefore, is that "perhaps [such acts] are not always morally wrong; but they are always morally significant." [5] It may be said, as we have already seen, that mating the king is of "such significance" that the relevant sort of elision is inadmissible; and yet, one would be bound to add, ". . . in the context of playing a game of chess." Apparently, D'Arcy is holding that the significance of the categories he has marked out holds *sans phrase* (or, as one might otherwise say, for human life as such). *If* one felt that the *moral* context was a distinct context from the financial or the prudential or the technical (but a restricted one), one might be inclined to construe D'Arcy's view as a view about morally serious issues *and,* consequently, that his thesis was false —since technical questions about what one does may easily ignore (specialized) moral issues (for instance, how much cyanide the living body can be made to absorb is a question that ignores the morally significant issue of poisoning). On the other hand, if one felt that the moral context covered all questions of human life and conduct, in the sense that questions of overriding values are always, in principle, relevant for rational agents, D'Arcy's thesis would have to be viewed as a form of moral essentialism— that, given man's nature, it is necessary to admit as morally relevant the characterization of all acts under D'Arcy's non-elidible act-descriptions and it is even conceptually wrong to ignore or obscure or eliminate any of these categories in the context of moral judgment. But we have already seen that there are no cognitive grounds on which to support a claim regarding normative human nature, and an appeal merely to the presumptive interests of prudential agents must prove both irrelevant and inadequate.

It is also to the point to observe that D'Arcy misleads us when he says that "to put forward this thesis is not to espouse any one particular ethical theory; people may concur in subscribing to it, but differ widely when they come to give a rationale of moral-species-terms [that is, terms like 'breaking a promise,' 'mayhem,' 'murder']." [6] He thinks that there need not be "unanimous agreement on every detail of the definition and identification and evaluation of all these species-terms." [7] But the claim is quite indecisive since, in spite of the range of possible disagreement that D'Arcy indicates, there will be, and can be (by his view), no defensible disagreement about the moral import of those terms *"into which* some sort of moral judgment is built" and about those terms, however factual and descriptive, that relate to "data *necessary* for reaching a sound [moral] verdict." [8] D'Arcy must be holding to some putatively unalterable code of moral classification that may be correctly posited for mankind, within whose limits (rather as in the Thomist doctrine of the relationship between natural law and positive law) *some* range of dispute is possible. But the thesis cannot be defended.

Consider, in this regard, D'Arcy's account of acts of omission. "A person is said to have omitted X," he holds, "if, and only if, (1) he did not do X, and (2) X was in some way expected of him." [9] That an act is "expected" may be established in two ways: "First, it may be expected because X is something that A usually does, or people usually do, in the situation in question. . . . Second, we also speak of A's not-doing-X as an omission when X is required of him by some rule with which he is expected to comply [moral or non-moral rule, precept, principle or the like]." [10] Finally, D'Arcy speaks of "immoral omissions" in three types of cases: "First, A deliberately let Y happen, when he should have prevented it; second, A did not do X, which he should have done, and the result was that Y happened; third, A did Z, which was incompatible with his doing X, and X was something which he was supposed to do." [11]

There are several telling things to be said about this account. For one, deeds and acts have been confused. It is certainly the case that if someone has omitted to do X, he has *done* something, namely, omitted to do X; but it is not at all usual (though it is possible) that his omission count as an *act*. Hence, it may well be that an omission cannot be judged as immoral unless it is suitably located in an appropriate context of moral responsibility and evaluation. Secondly, D'Arcy has himself provided, in speaking of so-called acts of omission, for cases in which morally relevant judgments are guided by conventional practices and expectations and *not* by considerations of what is essential, in any sense whatsoever, to human nature or manifests the kind of significance allegedly associated with non-elidible act-descriptions. But if the relevant omissions are omissions regarding acts and if moral censure depends here on conventional expectations, there is no reason to think—as far as the argument goes—that the unalterability of certain ranges of act-descriptions is not itself to be seen as relative to the conventional practices of particular societies. If we are censured for omissions regarding acts we are expected to perform—in either of the two senses D'Arcy provides (because, say, of habit or practice or rule)—what argument can be supplied to convince us that, when we are censured for the acts we *commit,* we are not censured for a breach of established practice or rule but rather for a violation of what is essential to human nature as such? There appears to be no tenable argument.

A third consideration is this: morally relevant acts, and omissions with respect to them, are (on D'Arcy's thesis) governed in some way by rules, precepts, and the like. In this respect, morality is, granting the thesis, rather like chess. The difficulties of imposing the game model on the moral domain aside, one cannot deny that games like chess are entirely conventional undertakings. Either, therefore, morality—as rule-governed—is similarly conventional or else the specifically moral rules of play are, in some way or other, derivable from human nature itself. The first alternative undermines D'Arcy's thesis about non-elidibility, since it is always possible to change the practices of a society; and the second alternative is, as we have already seen, quite indefensible.

The importance of the foregoing argument cannot be underestimated. For, what it entails is the possibility of radical reforms and changes in the most persistent and seemingly fundamental practices of human society. If D'Arcy's thesis is false, if terms denoting morally relevant acts and their consequences may, in principle, always be elided, then no moral categories of the relevant sort are unalterable. Those terms, like 'murder,' 'mayhem,' and 'deceit,' that have "some sort of moral judgment" built into them, may always be detached from such judgment and redefined as "purely factual and descriptive." And those terms, like 'kill,' 'maim,' and 'deceive,' alleged to be "purely factual and descriptive," may be freed from any aroma of moral import whatsoever; they may, in principle, cease to be relevant ("necessary," is D'Arcy's rather too strong claim) "for reaching a sound [moral] verdict." [12]

We may appreciate this if we see that terms like 'kill,' 'maim,' and 'deceive' are linked to the presumptive interests of prudential agents; it is regularly assumed, therefore, notably by utilitarians and egoists, that man's *presumptive* interests must be served in any viable *moral* program. But the implied argument is a *non sequitur*. The point is that the catalogue of act-descriptions to which we subscribe is conceptually bound to our valuational practices, both to positive appraisals of particular acts and to our sense that certain ranges of events must be appraised in certain serious ways. Our catalogue is simply the underside of our conventional morality: there is no room for unqualified debate about what rules or precepts or practices we are commited to, respecting our acts, once it is conceded that descriptions covering morally relevant acts cannot provide, beyond a certain point, for the elision of act and consequence; the concession is tantamount to the admission of governing moral rules. This is the reason, at one and the same time, why, *within* a moral convention, questions about right and wrong, obligation, duty, rights, justification, excuses, and the like are regularly settled as findings and why, with an eye to challenging the practices of a society, reformers appear to be misdescribing the palpable acts (and deeds) before us. The capitalist construes the expropriation of his property as theft; the Marxist zealot construes possession of private property as theft. Temple authorities regard adultery as a physical act; Jesus speaks of adultery in the heart. The evidence is conclusive, therefore, that the defense of a thesis like D'Arcy's —for good or for bad—is morally conservative and partisan, and that the admission of the elidibility of act and consequence is tantamount to providing, within the moral tradition itself, for revolutionary changes in our moral convictions and practice.

The problem goes deeper in fact. Not only the elision of act and consequence but also the individuation of acts and actions reflects variable convictions regarding normative (and, in particular, moral) values. And the import of this, linked with the rejection of cognitivism, is quite radical. It means, for instance, that history, as the record of the actions of men, cannot but be written from a partisan view or from the vantage of some relatively institutionalized network of act-descriptions—which, broadly speaking, comes to the same thing. For the historian, formulating what he believes to have been done by men, cannot avoid treating men as men (and not merely as occupying special roles or functions) and cannot, therefore, avoid describing what has happened as the acts of men (which requires attention to normative and, in particular, overriding values, in accord with some selection of which, systematic descriptions may be rendered). The mere characterization of events as acts and actions is the obverse side of our subscription to certain constitutive conventions (as of chess) or our recognition of certain regularized, purposive activities (as of building a house) or our adoption of certain normative values (as in judging another to have committed murder). But, inasmuch as moral considerations are overriding considerations, any act or action may be described or redescribed in morally relevant terms and, in that sense, on the argument given, act-descriptions will be unable to escape the imprint of a partisan conviction.

The force and scope of this conclusion may be judged readily enough by examining the much-debated, but seemingly remote, issue of whether explanation by reasons (to include, generously, the ascription of motives, intentions, purposes, reasons, and the like)` is or is not a species of explanation by causes. The connection with our own topic is fairly straightforward: for, the justification of actions (moral, legal, prudential, and the like) characteristically (though not exclusively) corresponds to an explanation by reasons, of such actions; and the individuation of acts and actions eligible for justification presupposes the institutions and conventions of a particular society. The question is something of a detour, however, and we shall drop it as soon as it allows us to clarify the issue of individuating actions.

Consider, then, these two fairly representative views on the question of reasons and causes. One holds that explanations by reasons are explanations of what one has done because of reasons one has *and* that one *has* reasons for acting if and only if having reasons causally affects one's acting. This is substantially the thesis of Donald Davidson for instance. On the other hand, one may say that the reason or motive for doing something "interprets" an action (rationalizes or justifies it)—explains it thus —but that the reason supplied cannot be said to be a cause of the action; such a thesis fails, to that extent, to face the question squarely whether the reason or motive supplied, when *had* by some agent, is a part of the cause of his action. Broadly speaking, this is the form for instance of G. E. M. Anscombe's account. Asked to supply a reason for one's turning on the light, Davidson considers one's *wanting* to turn it on; asked to supply a reason for someone's killing another, Miss Anscombe considers the *response,* "Because he killed my brother."

Now, it is generally assumed that actions designated in given contexts by widely different descriptions may be one and the same; and Davidson and Anscombe, though they hold diametrically opposed views, nevertheless agree that they may speak with confidence of one and the same action under significantly different descriptions. Davidson, for instance, says: "I flip the switch, turn on the light, and illuminate the room. Unbeknownst to me, I also alert a prowler to the fact that I am home. Here I do not do four things, but only one, of which four descriptions have been given." [13] And Miss Anscombe asks: "Are we to say that the man who (intentionally) moves his arm, operates the pump, replenishes the water-supply, poisons the inhabitants, is performing *four* actions? Or only one?" She answers: ". . . moving his arm up and down with his fingers round the pump handle *is,* in these circumstances, operating the pump; and, in these circumstances, it *is* replenishing the house water-supply; and, in these circumstances, it *is* poisoning the household." [14]

On the assumption underlying both Davidson's and Anscombe's accounts, however, certain difficulties present themselves. It seems plain that a man may intend to flip the switch without intending to turn on the light or without intending to illuminate the room or without intending to alert the prowler. And a man may intend to move his arm without intending to operate the pump or without intending to replenish the water-supply or without intending to poison the inhabitants. But if this is so, then intentions for particular actions are description-relative: one can have an intention for an action under one description without having a relevant intention for the *very same action* under another description. But if this is the case, then having an intention is not, as such, a cause of an action, if causes, as we seem to hold, are not description-relative. For, if they are held to be description-relative in the same sense, we should have to admit that a given intention might be both a cause and not a cause of the same action—which seems anomalous—and we should also lose a large part of the systematic advantage to be gained by vindicating the causal thesis.

Consider that having the intention of operating the pump explains moving one's arm up and down on the pump handle—explains it, as Miss Anscombe says, by interpreting the action, answers a certain question "Why?" [15] Such an intention cannot explain the action of poisoning the inhabitants, simply because, *ex hypothesi*, the relevant intention was not had by the agent and the intention the agent actually had does not relevantly bear on the action to be explained (on the description given). Yet, on the account given, the action of operating the pump and the action of poisoning the inhabitants are one and the same. So it appears that an explanation by reasons suitable and adequate for a given action, under one description, will not do at all for the very same action, under another description: one's intention to operate the pump doesn't explain the *action* of poisoning the inhabitants *at all,* in the sense of providing reasons for the action done, in whatever sense it does provide an explanation (by reasons) of moving one's arm up and down on the pump handle. It is, however, clear that if having the intention of operating the pump causally explains the action of operating the pump, it also contributes to the causal explanation of the poisoning of the inhabitants, since they are the same action: what is a part of the cause of operating the pump is a part of the cause of poisoning the inhabitants. But then, explanation by reasons cannot, as such, be a species of causal explanation, if a given intention that an agent has, enters into a causal explanation of a given action and, although *had,* cannot enter into a suitable and adequate explanation by reasons (or intentions or motives) of the very same action. This is the upshot of saying that explanations in terms of intentions and the like are description-relative and that explanations in terms of causes are not. For, the intention of operating the pump enters fully and properly into explanations of both sorts, respecting the action of operating the pump, but does not enter fully and properly into explanations of both sorts, respecting the poisoning of the inhabitants—*though they are one and the same action.* There must, therefore, be a sense in which a man may be said to *have* an intention, which explains his action, in a description-relative sense that is *not* a causal sense of 'have'; for, if the causal sense is the only eligible sense, then having the intention of operating the pump must enter into the explanation by *reasons* of the action of poisoning the inhabitants *if* it enters into the *causal* account of that action. But this is obviously not true for the case before us.

It will, then, not be possible to hold, with Davidson, that "if rationalization is . . . a species of causal explanation, then justification . . . is at least one differentiating property [of those causal explanations that identify reasons had as causes]." [16] For, following our example, in spite of the fact that having the intention of operating the pump both rationalizes and causally explains moving one's arm up and down on the pump handle, it does not rationalize, or explain by reasons, poisoning the inhabitants—which, on the thesis, is the very same action. The justificatory function of the rationalization cannot be "one differentiating property" of *such causal explanations,* since, though it is indeed had, it has absolutely no bearing on the rationalization of *that action* under the description of poisoning the inhabitants. It is one thing to hold that, since the agent does not, *ex hypothesi, have* the intention of poisoning the inhabitants, that intention is not a cause of the action (under any description we may choose); it is quite another to hold that, although the intention to operate the pump is one the agent has, it is quite irrelevant to the rationalization of the very action it causally affects. Why should it be, we may well ask, if explanation by reasons is a species of explanation by causes and if having a reason or intention for an action done is part of the cause of the action, that the intention an agent admittedly has may not be admissible in an explanation (by reasons) of the very action (under some description) of which it is part of the cause? Why does not the alleged generic property of such explanations—that they are of a causal sort—not insure an explanatory role in all relevant rationalizations of precisely the factor (the intention had) that plays the chief role in openly causal explanations? I confess I cannot see the answer, unless it is to deny that explanation by reasons *is* a species of explanation by causes—though without denying, at the same time, that the intentions an agent has may well enter in a causal explanation of a given action. On the condition, then—agreed to by both Davidson and Anscombe —that one and the same action may be identified under the sort of divergent descriptions of which both have provided specimens, explanation by reasons cannot be shown to be a species of causal explanation.

Still, it may be possible to save the causal thesis by adjusting the claim that single actions may be identified under alternative descriptions. It may, for example, be possible to hold that the action (or act) of operating the pump caused the action (or act) of poisoning the inhabitants, that what we have here are distinct acts and not merely distinct descriptions of the same act. On such a reading, the intention of operating the pump explains, consistently with the causal thesis, the action of moving one's arm on the pump; furthermore, the action of operating the pump may, consistently with the thesis, be said to cause the act of poisoning the inhabitants. The original intention need not relevantly bear on an explanation (by reasons) of *that* action, since, *ex hypothesi,* the action is distinct from the other and is not caused by a relevant intention (in the sense in which Davidson speaks of a "primary reason").[17] The difficulty with such a view is, quite obviously, that it depends, like the view it replaces, on some unformulated principle for individuating actions—one, in fact, that appears to be entirely *ad hoc.* For, wherever we are threatened with the paradoxes already mustered, we resolve them by distinguishing what otherwise may appear to be one and the same action under alternative descriptions. We may patch the view as we please, but it seems unreasonable to hold that, for any range of relevant descriptions, alternative descriptions never (unless they are clearly synonymous) pick out the same act or action. It is also, I think, entirely counter-intuitive to say, for example, that the act (or action) of moving the arm up and down on the pump handle *caused the act* (or *action*) of operating the pump. The relationship between the two is simply too intimate. A better view is that the act (or action) of operating the pump entails the act (or action) of moving the arm up and down, though this in itself cannot resolve our question; we should still need to decide how to individuate such acts (or actions) and how to determine such entailments.

A second solution is superficially simpler. We might distinguish between acts (or actions) and their consequences (not to be construed as actions). Thus, for instance, the intention of operating the pump would explain, consistently with the causal thesis, the action of moving the arm up and down on the pump handle; but it would not, and would not need to, explain the action of poisoning the inhabitants, since (on the hypothesis) *that* is a consequence of the action and not an action itself. The difficulty facing this thesis is, however, quite decisive. Not only are the acknowledged problems concerning individuation unresolved (and the solution to them presupposed) but there is, as we have already argued, no clearly compelling reason why what, under one description, is characterized as an action and its consequences may not, under another, be redescribed as itself an action. For instance, the description of the action of operating the pump and its consequence, the poisoning of the inhabitants, may be elided into a new description, that of the action (or act) of poisoning the inhabitants (by operating the pump, of course). To deny this is to be driven back to Eric D'Arcy's views. The difficulties adduced, then, demonstrate that it will do no good to attempt a direct answer to the question whether explanation by reasons is a species of explanation by causes or how the one is related to the other without a deeper analysis of what it is to be an action.

I have, finally, one essential clue to offer respecting the problem of individuating acts and actions. Consider that, in the law, a man may be charged with having committed multiple criminal *acts* when what he has done, under ordinary circumstances, would probably be regarded as a single *action*. Imagine, for instance, that a man has walked a few steps on a given path. He may have trespassed; he may have entered an officially restricted area; he may have set off public alarms without cause or justification; he may have endangered the security of the country; he may have been spying. It is conceivable that such a man may be tried, as we say, on five counts (rather as a man may be charged with striking an officer and resisting arrest, by performing what appears to be the single action of punching a policeman in the nose). The point to be emphasized is simply that, in an institutionalized society, there will normally appear conventions for the counting of distinct acts—where the principles of individuation are clearly and principally guided by considerations of responsibility, liability, scoring and winning in games, and the like, that answer to the values that conventionally obtain in such a society. It does not seem that the individuation allowed is at all determined by considerations of a causal sort or even of an intentional sort, although both causes and intentions may relevantly enter as criteria bearing on the individuation of acts. In fact, to hold that a man has, say, committed five distinct acts for which he is criminally liable is, so it seems, to say no more than that he is liable for five enumerable charges; and if the law should change, it is quite possible that the number of charges would change without any change at all in the given causal and intentional factors. The trouble, in a word, is that precisely where the individuation of acts is relatively clearcut—as by way of legal conventions or in accord with the rules of a game— the principles involved have less to do with a resolution of our question regarding explanation by causes than they do with ascribing responsibility and counting the significant features of whatever has occurred.[18]

But if this is true in the most formalized contexts in which we speak of human acts and actions, there is good reason to think that similar (though more informal) considerations guide our individuation of acts and actions in relatively informal discourse as well. On the suggestion given, the individuation of acts, in fairly formalized contexts, simply does not require us, except in the most generous sense of making grammatical reference (consistent with all sorts of alternative individuating locutions), to individuate, among occurrent phenomena, actions that will be reinterpreted as distinct acts. Individuation, here, seems to have the sole purpose of permitting, in context, the counting of certain relevant items that may be assigned to a human agent: change the purpose, having nothing necessarily to do with causal issues, and one changes the count. It is also worth remarking that the contexts in which individuation is highly developed are precisely the ones in which explanation by reasons does not always require that reasons relevantly advanced be reasons that the agent *has,* in a sense favorable to either causal explanations or explanations in terms of actual intentions. For instance, in the Wild West, a man's act may have been properly described as an act of self-defense rather than as murder (firing after another man has drawn his gun) in spite of the fact that he knew he was faster and deliberately provoked his opponent into drawing first. The justifying reasons clearly need not be reasons that the agent *had* in acting as he did. Again, an accidental play in bridge —distractedly playing one card for another—may justify the taking of a trick, regardless of the player's intention. It appears, therefore, that what we call actions form a logically mixed category, with respect to which explanations of different sorts overlap and intersect to some extent: the logic of justificatory reasons appears to be substantially different from the logic of the reasons that an agent has in acting as he does, and the logic of the latter appears to be significantly different from the logic of the causal explanation of his action. Explanation by reasons is, characteristically, the rationalization or justification of actions, offered in terms of relevant norms, whether of established games or regularized skills or technical endeavors or prudential interests or *ad hoc* conventions or overriding values assumed to obtain. Explanation in terms of the reasons an agent actually has, moves bifocally in accord with justification and in accord with causal explanation. The difference between the latter sorts of explanation is simply that justification concerns rules or rule-like regularities only (with respect to which, breaches of operative rules are not physically impossible) and that causal explanation concerns causal laws (with respect to which, whatever is contrary to a valid law is, even if it be unknown, physically impossible). To separate the two is to resolve, at a stroke, the paradoxes of individuation and explanation already noted. Explanation in terms of the reasons an agent *has,* then, may favor the pattern of causal explanation exclusively (in the sense in which the reason had, accounts for the occurrence of the event, though it does not serve to justify what has happened—is not linked to justificatory considerations) or it may favor the pattern of justification primarily (in the sense in which, waiving any possible causal role, the reasons said to be had by the agent are, when accepted, reasons that justify what he has done—are linked to justificatory considerations) or it may combine considerations of both sorts. The promising key seems, therefore, to lie more with the points of contacts and difference among these alternatives than with the prospects of subsuming one under the other. But the conclusion cannot be burked that the description and individuation of acts and actions—hence, their appraisal and justification as well— are substantially dependent on the conventional norms and institutions prevailing in given societies. And this confirms again that we cannot expect to demonstrate that moral judgments may be construed as findings, in a sense stronger than the relativity of institutionalized norms would support; for, norms subtend alternative networks of act-descriptions, and the categories of moral assessment and those of the relevant description of human behavior are simply coordinate concepts within a common system.

CHAPTER 8

Convictions, Rules, and Principles

IT IS OFTEN PIOUSLY MAINTAINED that, in spite of the conceptual puzzles of moral philosophy, human societies have always exhibited striking agreement about moral values. The claim is not so much true or false as vacuous. If, for instance, Roman fathers, at one time, held an apparently justified right of life and death over their sons without an obligation to account for the exercise of that right, whereas in no contemporary Western society can a remotely similar right be found or defended, the evident difference may be muted by an assumption of the evolutionary nature of moral consciousness. The trouble is that the evolutionary thesis is itself either an assumption of some normal moral *development* or *progress* proper to man (which is, then, merely a version of the doctrine of normative human nature historicized) or else an assumption that variant moral convictions (adjusted, so it will be emphasized, to the detailed differences of the lives of different societies) are universally tested by appeal to some ulterior and comprehensive principle—such as the notorious principle of the "survival of the fittest" (which allegedly demonstrates, then, that men after all do agree strikingly about moral values).[1] There are other strategies, of course, by which to coax along this confidence in the relative uniformity of the moral consciousness of the race. One can appeal straightforwardly, against all opposition, to some alleged Law of Nature underlying obvious moral variations (whether, for instance, Hobbesian or Thomistic) or to some doctrine of normative human nature itself; one can appeal to some allegedly Ideal Observer[2] (who, in any relevant sense, must subscribe to some version of cognitivism) or to a revealed doctrine or to some cognitivist doctrine directly; one can appeal to anthropologically, psychologically, or sociologically documented universal needs or desires[3] (which, again, is nothing but the thesis of normative human nature warmed over); one can insist that any defensible moral program include the admitted, presumptive interests of prudential agents (which confuses the moral and the prudential, obscures the problem of defending ulterior moral principles, begs the question, and at least dimly assumes a normative human nature). In a word, in the face of widespread variations in moral conviction, the thesis that apparently significant divergence confirms a common sensibility depends either on the partisan preference of some criterion for discriminating true and false sensibility or on the adoption of one of a number of doctrines already shown to be untenable.[4]

This is not to say that man is infinitely plastic, although the limits of his plasticity are extremely difficult to fix, increasingly so in a technological era that prides itself on altering both his environment and his physique and disposition. But it is crucial to observe that a specification of the putative plasticity, or of the limits of the plasticity, of man is *not*—any more than a specification of the presumptive interests of a prudential agent—equivalent to a moral program. For one thing, quite incompatible moral programs may be compatible with man's plasticity (depraved and saintly lives, for instance); and for another, the preference of one such program over another clearly must depend on an ulterior principle. This is nowhere more obvious than in the enormously influential tradition of utilitarianism and, particularly, in the details of J. S. Mill's *Utilitarianism*—which may provide us, therefore, with an instructive paradigm for a very wide range of doctrines of "rational" morality, eudaimonism, moral teleology, and the like.

Subtleties and variations of particular versions aside, all utilitarian theories must hold either that men "by nature" desire certain ends only ("goods") that form the basis of the utilitarian program, or are "rational" only when they pursue the utilitarian program in accord with certain prominent desires, or the utilitarian program itself, however justified, is at least compatible with certain prominent desires and the plasticity of man. Jeremy Bentham oscillates between the first two views[5] and Mill, between the second and third. But the first is clearly false, for any specifiable desires—certainly, for the desires to pursue pleasure and avoid pain (by *any* non-tautological theory of pleasure and pain). And the second, as we have already argued, conflates the terms 'rational' and 'moral' and commits us, to some putatively normative human nature. The third, as I have suggested, is simply either irrelevant to the selection of a moral principle or trivial, in the sense that even to propose an admittedly evil principle is to consider its viability. But the third alternative obliges us also to consider a profound and common difficulty facing all metamoral theories. Consider, then, Mill's proof of the principle of utility. As far as I know, it has not been forcefully argued that Mill actually does not avail himself of the alleged proof and says a great many things which conclusively show that he never subscribed to it, on any of the alternative readings that have been advanced. "The sole evidence," Mill says in *Utilitarianism,*[6] "it is possible to produce that anything is desirable is that people do actually desire it." It can be demonstrated, I believe, that Mill held that desirability, in any fair sense offered for this remark, is neither a necessary nor a sufficient condition of goodness. The implications are considerable.

Mill holds that "happiness has made out its title as *one* of the ends of conduct, and consequently one of the criteria of morality" (in that people actually do desire happiness).[7] But he admits that the utilitarian principle requires "not only that people desire happiness, but that they never desire anything else." This explains why he spends the time he does reconciling "the desire of virtue" with "the desire of happiness" and why he spends a disproportionate amount of time reconciling justice and utility.[8] In principle, it would be sufficient to defeat Mill to demonstrate that virtue or justice or similar "desirable" ends are not conceptually dependent on the goal of happiness. Every utilitarian program is similarly vulnerable. But there is a more telling difficulty confronting Mill's utilitarianism, namely, that the greatest happiness principle is espoused by Mill *without regard to, and even contrary to, the promptings of desire.*

Consider the following remark:

> . . . will, in the beginning, is entirely produced by desire; including in that term the repelling influence of pain as well as the attractive one of pleasure. . . . How can the will to be virtuous, where it does not exist in sufficient force, be implanted or awakened? Only by making the person *desire* virtue—by making him think of it in a pleasurable light, or of its absence in a painful one. It is by associating the doing right with pleasure, or the doing wrong with pain, or by eliciting and impressing and bringing home to the person's experience the pleasure naturally involved in the one or the pain in the other, that it is possible to call forth that will to be virtuous which, when confirmed, acts without any thought of either pleasure or pain.[9]

Mill is here concerned with the psychology of influence and education: a man may be induced to behave virtuously in so far as he may be made to associate the presence (or absence) of virtue with pleasure (or pain). But beyond this, Mill obviously *knows antecedently that virtue is good* and therefore that a man *ought* to be induced to construe virtue as pleasant. The essential paradox of utilitarianism, that it "maintains not only that virtue is to be desired, but that it is to be desired disinterestedly, for itself"[10] is resolvable only on this view. For Mill admits that virtue is to be desired "even although, in the individual instance, it should not produce those other desirable consequences which it tends to produce, and on account of which it is held to be virtue." [11] In fact, he says, "Virtue, according to the utilitarian doctrine, is not naturally and originally part of the end, but it is capable of becoming so. . . ." [12] Now, Mill nowhere means that it is psychologically impossible to view vice with pleasure (think of the Marquis de Sade). He must therefore know not only that virtue *can* be associated with pleasure but that it *ought* to be so associated. It follows that Mill does not construe virtue to be a criterion of morality on the grounds of desire, though *any* would-be criterion must be psychologically compatible with desire. Virtue must be capable of being desired, but Mill everywhere insists that the wrong things are often desired.

These considerations oblige us to examine more closely the central maneuver in Mill's reconciliation of justice and utility. "That a feeling is bestowed on us by Nature," Mill declares, "does not necessarily legitimate all its promptings." [13] Now, the "feeling" of justice Mill construes rather as originating with an "instinct," what he sometimes characterizes as a "natural feeling of resentment." He means by this, obviously, since he speaks of "promptings" produced by this feeling, that, by nature, we have a persistent desire to revenge ourselves for hurts suffered. The feeling of justice itself Mill holds to be this "animal desire to repel or retaliate a hurt or damage to oneself or to those with whom one sympathizes . . . moralized by being made co-extensive with the demands of social good." It may well be that justice, *so* construed, is compatible with utilitarianism. But Mill has surely admitted that, by nature, men desire revenge for hurts suffered and that not all of the "promptings" of this natural feeling are morally legitimate. Consequently, desirability is not a sufficient condition of the moral goodness of revenge; and the correction of that "instinct" in accord "with the demands of social good" must be vindicated on the grounds of knowledge of what one ought to desire. If it is conceivable that a race of men be so depraved as not to desire "the greatest happiness," Mill would appear ready to correct, and (he thinks) be justified in correcting, their behavior. If this is so, then desirability in the relevant sense is not even a necessary condition of goodness—though, to be sure, any *effective* moral program must be capable of engaging desire.

The main feature of Mill's account is that desire is capable of being, and ought to be, *morally trained*. But of course, if this is so, then desirability, in any sense compatible with Mill's original proof of the utilitarian principle, cannot possibly serve as the criterion of morality. We desire revenge by *nature*, but we ought to desire justice (and we can be trained to). We desire virtue, Mill thinks, and though it "is not as universal . . . it is as authentic a fact as the desire of happiness." [14] Even if this be granted, Mill insists that "not only" is it "to be desired, but . . . it is to be desired disinterestedly, for itself," that anything less would not be compatible with utilitarianism. Once again, then, an established desire ought to be adjusted in the interests of morality.

Of course, a very important and honest concession has been made here by Mill. Though virtue is desired, it is not universally desired; nevertheless, we know that virtue is normatively desirable. It is easy to see that Mill would not, and could not, hold that the normative desirability of virtue is determined by its actually being desired. Some things are desired, he has admitted, that are not adequately moral; and some things are moral that men, by nature, are not inclined to desire—but may be trained to desire. Think of a predominantly or entirely depraved race. Would virtue, or justice, on Mill's grounds, be the same or different for this race? There can be no question that Mill looked to a science of value and believed his discoveries would be binding on all men.[15] But there is no way in which he could support his view on the strength of the original proof. The depraved society clearly would not desire the greatest happiness or disinterested virtue or justice. Nevertheless, these things are known to be the criteria of morality, to be morally worth desiring.

Again, Mill's concessions regarding the greatest happiness principle are considerable. He says quite frankly that "the ultimate sanction . . . of all morality (external motives apart) [is] a subjective feeling in our minds . . . the conscientious feelings of mankind." [16] But he admits at once that "this feeling in most individuals is much inferior in strength to their selfish feelings, and is often wanting altogether." Nevertheless, "to those who have it, it possesses all the characters of a natural feeling"; and this "conviction," Mill declares, "is the ultimate sanction of the greatest happiness morality."

We must be careful here, because, in speaking of sanctions, Mill is speaking not primarily of what justifies the principle of utility but rather of what must make the utilitarian program (as any would-be moral program) effective. Still, in speaking of sanctions, he concedes that selfish desires dominate over "conscientious" desires, that in some natures "the conscientious feelings of mankind" are altogether lacking. Apart from the educative possibilities we have already seen Mill to be encouraged by, he admits that these deficient souls could only be made to respond to external sanctions. Perhaps so. But has he not, in the process, admitted that the disinterested desire of the happiness of "the aggregate of all persons" [17] is not actually felt by all and is known to be good regardless of this fact? So it is that Mill positively rejoices in insisting that the "powerful natural sentiment" of "the social feelings of mankind . . . will constitute the strength of the utilitarian morality . . . *once the general happiness is recognized as the ethical standard.*" [18] Clearly, Mill does not draw his principle from the actual desires of men, but is concerned rather to plan to use the patterns of human psychology to further his moral program.

This, I think, is the sense of Mill's otherwise puzzling remark, that, though "the moral feelings are not innate but acquired, they are not for that reason the less natural." [19] So he speaks of "properly cultivated moral natures," [20] "every rightly brought up human being." [21] The paradox of the proof of the principle of utility is nowhere more evident than here. For Mill, in his effort to maintain that "neither pains nor pleasures are homogeneous," [22] that "some *kinds* of pleasure are more desirable and more valuable than others," [23] is inevitably driven to disregard the actual desires of men as a guide to the criteria of morality. "It may be projected," Mill considers,

> that many who are capable of the higher pleasures occasionally, under the influence of temptation, postpone them to the lower. But this is quite compatible with a full appreciation of the intrinsic superiority of the higher. Men often, from infirmity of character, make their election for the nearer good, though they know it to be the less valuable. . . . But I do not believe that those who undergo this very common change, voluntarily choose the lower . . . pleasures in preference to the higher. I believe that before they devote themselves exclusively to the one, they have already become incapable of the other.[24]

Quite so. But then, precisely, Mill has the knowledge of the higher good in his back pocket all the time and never needs to consult actual desires. Those who prefer the lower to the higher cannot have chosen of their own volition. "Human beings have faculties more elevated than the animal appetites, and when once made conscious of them," Mill declares, "do not regard anything as happiness which does not include their gratification." [25] Anyone who does not subscribe to this view has not been "made conscious of them." "And if the fool, or the pig," he continues, "is of a different opinion, it is because they only know their own side of the question." [26] So it must be misleading to consult the desires of mankind at large, and it is superfluous to consult the desires of those who know what is good. "Better to be Socrates dissatisfied than a fool satisfied";[27] but *to be Socrates is to know what is good for human nature*, what it is human beings *ought* to, though unreliably now, desire.

Mill, then, is essentially a eudaimonist, who claims to know what the desires of men ought to be and therefore can well afford to be critical of their actual desires. But to say that this is the sense in which Mill offers his proof of the principle of utility in terms of desire is to change defeat into victory by an act of christening and to disregard utterly Mill's own very deep mistrust of the recognizable desires of the run of mankind. By Mill's own arguments, then, desirability (in any non-question-begging sense) is neither a necessary nor a sufficient condition of moral goodness, and no consultation of men's actual desires is, for him, ever in the least decisive regarding what is good. The only reason for attending to the fact that people are known to desire happiness, virtue, and justice is, simply, that it provides important educative possibilities for enlarging and reinforcing our commitment to morality.

The importance of these problems cannot be exaggerated. Utilitarianism, regardless of its various specifications of the goods of human life and regardless of its various specifications of the point at which utilitarian criteria are to be brought to bear on the assessment of human conduct and institutions, is inherently either a conceptual dangler, a partisan vision of normative human life, or else an indefensible dogma of a cognitivist or essentialist sort. Moreover, if the arguments bearing on utilitarianism be sustained, then every metamoral theory of a teleological sort will exhibit precisely the same weakness. Construe the morality of acts or institutions solely in terms of allegedly intrinsic or ideal goods and one is bound to ask for a justification for the overriding preference of such goods—*whatever they may be.* The alternatives, then, just specified, are seen to be the only eligible ones. Furthermore, it turns out that every teleological theory considered in this light may just as readily be construed as a theory of a deontological sort, for every metamoral theory is ultimately concerned with overriding values. Given the sense of 'ought' adjusted to the moral domain (as a ranking predicate respecting overriding values) there remains no satisfactory way to distinguish the use of 'good' in teleological metamoral theories, and of 'ought,' in deontological theories.[28] Only a defensible cognitivism or essentialism could have provided a basis for the required distinction. The import of this conclusion converges with that of an earlier argument respecting so-called duties to self and to others; for here we see that ulterior teleological theories by which to assess the conventional morality of any society must correspond with what, in at least certain traditions, are termed duties to self—a concern that (as we have argued) is inherently open to judgments no stronger than appreciative judgments. Even the vision of a brotherhood of self-fulfilling selves, of course, cannot escape this dependency on ulterior appreciative judgments. The upshot is that, in the context of metamoral disputes, the terminological preference of 'good' or 'right' or 'ought' or 'duty' or the like as the primitive moral predicate is—patently false doctrines aside—ultimately stylistic.

The developing difficulty of sorting out metamoral principles as teleological or deontological (which does not signify any difficulty in distinguishing one metamoral theory from another) may be pressed further. Disregard for the moment the questions already raised about the selection of overriding values and consider only questions regarding the second sort of distinction mentioned, in terms of which utilitarianism may vary—that is, regarding the specified point at which utilitarian criteria are to be brought to bear in assessing human conduct and institutions. The central quarrel, in effect a family quarrel among utilitarians, concerns the difference between, and the comparative tenability of, so-called act- and rule-utilitarianism. The issue is a vexed one but instructive; it is, I think, best introduced in historical terms.

W. D. Ross, it will be remembered, had, in his *The Right and the Good*,[29] decisively challenged all efforts to make act-utilitarianism a comprehensive principle on which to judge ethical issues. The reason one ought to keep a promise, he explained, is simply that one had made a promise, not consideration of the possible consequences (bonific or optimific) of doing so. He added also that the question of consequences did not even arise as a *prima facie* consideration and that, if it were raised, it could not be said to be self-evident that doing what was right would produce bonific or optimific consequences. His arguments, direct and telling, collected the scattered objections of an earlier tradition, notably incorporating the views of Joseph Butler, and were accepted by more recent utilitarian-minded theorists not prepared to accept his intuitionism.

This was a considerable tribute. Much current utilitarianism tends to agree that, following a distinction advanced by John Rawls, utilitarian considerations are not eligible in offering reasons for right acts.[30] Rawls points out that one cannot defend his keeping a promise because it would have good consequences— the outcome would be that one might defend his breaking a promise because it too might have good consequences; but he insists that, though an act cannot be so defended, a practice can be (and reasonably may be required to be) defended on utilitarian grounds. This is what is meant by rule-utilitarianism. In fact, Rawls offers the ingenious (and convincing) explanation that "there are obvious utilitarian advantages in having a practice which denies to the promisor, as a defense, any general appeal to the utilitarian principle in accordance with which the practice itself may be justified." [31] Rawls thereby outflanks, by adoption, the anti-utilitarian arguments of Ross. It is, of course, also possible to prefer the act-utilitarian position—which is J. J. C. Smart's choice, for instance.[32] But then, the difficulties uncovered by Mill's account will remain unanswerable in any case.

The question needs to be asked whether Rawls' maneuver, attractive in itself, is put forward in a defensible form and, further, whether it is in principle possible to formulate it adequately. To state the same in another way, Is act-utilitarianism altogether indefensible and can rule-utilitarianism be sufficiently distinguished from act-utilitarianism? I should answer both these questions, No. The importance of the counter-argument is not so much that it exhibits certain difficulties inherent in rule-utilitarianism as that it suggests the impossibility of formulating a comprehensive and persuasive principle on which all ethical judgments can be defended.

The strategy I adopt is this. First, identify certain kinds of cases in which utilitarian considerations are directly relevant. If these can be supported, Rawls' restriction about the eligibility of such considerations falls. Next, consider Rawls' own formulation of rule-utilitarianism and show why these kinds of cases cannot be managed on his account and, further, why it is inherently impossible to distinguish rule-utilitarianism from act-utilitarianism. Finally, consider how, if the matter were pressed, it might be shown to be extremely difficult to distinguish rule- or act-utilitarianism from intuitionism (at least of the deontological sort advocated by Ross).

I ask you to consider the case of the thalidomide babies. One prominent ethical teaching holds that we ought not to take the life of another human being. The doctrine is to be construed, and may reasonably be shown, to provide that certain excuses and exceptions and the like are part of the sense of the governing practice. Killing enemy soldiers during wartime, self-defense, and accidental homicide are all comprehended within the practice of not taking another's life. The killing of thalidomide babies is not obviously provided for in the practice (in the sense in which a rule would provide for its defensibility). One cannot simply say that the killing of these babies is *right* as one can say that the killing of the enemy is *right*. I think we are prepared to concede, however, that though—according to the teaching—it is wrong to take another's life, it might have very significant bonific (or even optimific) consequences to end the lives of such terribly handicapped infants; that, furthermore, since such an act would have such *good* consequences (and avoid such evil consequences) it might therefore be right. I am not saying that it would be right or wrong but only that we would regard the debate as *eligible*. But, if it were eligible, it would follow that utilitarian considerations are *sometimes* open in the defense of an act that otherwise falls under a practice defining what is right. I am saying that if we construe a practice as open to utilitarian defense, we should be obliged to admit such a defense for acts as well. I am not insisting that practices require utilitarian defense.

I am arguing from what are known as "hard cases." Breaking a promise under certain extraordinary circumstances, the killing of a moral monster, the taking of life of thalidomide babies, acts of mercy killing, and the like *sometimes* may be so construed that *utilitarian considerations rather than the provisions implicit in the practice itself* may be entitled to a hearing. Under such circumstances, Rawls' distinction between justifying an act and justifying a practice founders. Furthermore, we may suspect that the differences between utilitarian consequences and provisions inherent in an allegedly given practice cannot be easily formulated; and that, if they cannot, the distinction between intuitionist (deontological) grounds for particular acts and utilitarian grounds cannot be sharply drawn either. The suspicion is considerably strengthened, it may be added, by recalling that we have already established that descriptions of acts and consequences are always, in principle, elidible.

Consider now Rawls' own account. One of the requirements for the defense of rule-utilitarianism, as he rightly sees, is the provision of an adequate conception of a rule. Rawls rejects one possible way of construing a rule, that is, as a summary of past decisions and acts that may serve as a guide for future conduct. The difficulty with this view is that, in principle, utilitarian considerations will have been employed in judging the individual cases on which the rule itself is based; Ross' objections will then be unanswerable. On the summary interpretation, utilitarianism must always take the form of act-utilitarianism. Also, it will not be possible to formulate what is to count as a breach of the rule. Rawls' own preference is for what he calls "the practice conception," that is, the view that "rules are pictured as defining a practice." [33] As he says further (and fairly): "it is essential to the notion of a practice that the rules are publicly known and understood as definitive." [34] This is not to say that excuses and exceptions and the like are not eligible but rather that they are provided for in the formulation of the full rule. From this point of view, appeal to an exception is an appeal to a rule and not to utilitarian considerations; the latter apply to the justification of the practice, never to acts that fall under a practice. One sees, therefore, that, in an important sense rule-utilitarianism is, as formulated, a mixed metamoral theory. For one thing, it will incorporate some sort of formalism; and, for another, it will be obliged to disregard potential discrepancies resulting from applying its own utilitarian criterion to *both* conforming to a practice and departing from it in particular acts. To revise its rules always on the basis of such considerations will be tantamount to erasing the difference between act- and rule-utilitarianism.[35]

It needs to be said that Rawls is, in a way, the first to notice the strain of this second conception of rules. He does say, for instance:

> utilitarians would be inclined to hold that some reliance on people's *good sense* and some concession to *hard cases* is necessary. They would hold that a practice is justified by serving the interests of those who take part in it; and as with any set of rules there is understood a background of circumstances under which it is expected to be applied and which need not—indeed which *cannot*—be fully stated. Should these circumstances change, then *even if there is no rule* which provides for the case, it may still be in accordance with the practice that one be released from one's obligation. But this sort of defense allowed by a practice must not be confused with the general option to weigh each particular case on utilitarian grounds. . . .[36]

I have italicized the important phrases, the phrases that show us that act- and rule-utilitarianism cannot be sharply distinguished and, even that (Ross') intuitionism and utilitarianism cannot be sharply distinguished. Though Rawls sees a possible objection to rule-utilitarianism, he does not think it is a telling one. But he is mistaken, since his admission is tantamount to a denial that there is any formulable criterion for segregating "summary" rules from "practice" rules.

Hard cases, like the case of the thalidomide babies, are not clearly subsumable under the rule defining a practice; they constitute a challenge to any formulated rule—that is their precise contribution. If one were to hold that hard cases are comprehended under a practice, even if not under a rule defining a practice (as Rawls says), rule-utilitarianism would fall and we would have to admit that utilitarian considerations at times apply directly to the judging of particular acts. Alternatively put, if no adequate rule can in principle be formulated for a given practice, then (without raising any questions whatsoever about the proper account of what a rule is) it would not be possible to distinguish completely between act-utilitarianism and rule-utilitarianism. *A fortiori,* there would be no rule for deciding which were the hard cases in which utilitarian considerations would apply and which were ordinary cases where (following Ross) they would not apply. In short, what Rawls chooses to call "good sense" in judging "hard cases" may, in the absence of rules governing acts (granting, with him, the inappropriateness of utilitarian reasons in defending particular acts), be just as readily construed in intuitionist terms (in Ross' manner) as in terms of practices defended on utilitarian grounds. Otherwise, not granting what Ross and Rawls both concede, particular cases may be judged in accord with the precepts of act-utilitarianism.

An intuitionist like Ross might in fact very well claim that taking the life of a thalidomide baby was right, that it was *prima facie* right not to allow such senseless handicap and likelihood of suffering. By such a move, he would absorb allegedly utilitarian considerations into his own view. The reasons a utilitarian might give for judging an *act* or a *practice* might, by an intuitionist, be construed in terms of the characteristic *proper-ties* that right *acts* possess. There would then be no practice, in any sense independently formulable, to be defended at all—nothing but the acts themselves, which may exhibit a significant uniformity. Formalists about rules, of course, could offer their own analogue of rule-utilitarianism.[37]

The issue may be somewhat further clarified by considering typical moral rules, for instance, "Lying is wrong." It is instructive that although, in an obvious sense, it is a tautology, few would subscribe to it without qualification. I am not suggesting that all similar rules are tautologies. A good number are (and a good many may be equivocally construed), though Kant, for one, mentions the precept, "One ought to will that all his faculties should be developed." [38] If such be allowed, then not all would-be moral rules are tautologies. But "Lying is wrong" may obviously be read as a tautology and, nevertheless, people are reluctant to subscribe to it. We may well ask, how could they understand the rule and, without contradiction, fail to assent to it? And what is the implication of demurring? The outcome will affect other familiar precepts such as, "Poverty is evil," "War is wrong," "Suicide is wrong," "Sexual perversity is wrong"; it will affect also all metamoral theories that rely on the admission of moral rules that mediate between particular acts and overriding justificatory principles.

Clearly, if people disagree about "Lying is wrong," they cannot be viewing the rule in the same sense. If he claims that "Lying is wrong" cannot possibly be upset as a moral rule, we must suppose that one is drawing attention to the fact that the rule is a tautology. Possibly, he would explain that "Lying is wrong" means "Saying in a morally reprehensible way what one believes to be false is morally reprehensible." On the other hand, if he claims that it is not true that lying is always wrong, we must suppose that he is not in the least concerned with the tautological character of that rule. Possibly, he would explain that not all the cases *you* might consider cases of lying are properly so labeled. Or, that, though genuine cases of lying are morally wrong in so far as they are cases of lying, conduct cannot be judged in a morally appropriate way solely in terms of lying, even when lying is a consideration. The issue is a general one, and the demurrer applies to murder, promises, debts, and all similar categories.

There appear to be at least three distinct elements to be sorted out here: the import of the tautological rule itself; the grounds for judging whether this or that is, properly, a case of lying; and the grounds for judging whether this or that case of lying is, properly, morally wrong. Since one may acknowledge that "Lying is wrong" is a tautology and still admit the eligibility of the latter two issues, it must be the case that the rule is not very intimately connected with arguments supporting particular moral judgments. We must suppose, that is, that particular actions may be antecedently described in morally neutral terms and that we may debate their classification as instances of lying. Clearly, the rule "Lying is wrong" will always be superfluous to such debates. On the other hand, we must suppose that any action judged to be a genuine case of lying may yet have morally redeeming features; that, though it may have been wrong in so far as it was lying, yet it may not have been "simply" or "wholly" or "really" wrong. In a word, we treat the tautology conditionally; that is, we normally do not apply verdict-like predicates like 'wrong' to any action solely on the strength of such fractional categories as lying, contract-breaking, cheating, murder, or promise-breaking. It is, of course, illuminating to note that we *do* apply *legal* predicates in this fractional way; but then, precisely, legal considerations, like prudential and medical considerations, are not, as such, occupied with overriding values, but are concerned rather with certain technical goods. To say that lying is not always wrong is, by this view, to admit the tautological principle but to point to the conditional use of the moral predicate 'wrong.' We may schematize this as follows: "Lying is wrong. . . ." Alternatively put, the remark comes to this: "A lie is a lie, but it may sometimes be justified"—which is, in effect, to subsume some cases of lying under one or more comprehensive rules, themselves open to dispute, reform, rejection along the lines already indicated. The upshot is that we cannot affirm the autonomy or adequacy of any particular rule as far as the rendering of moral verdicts is concerned; however wrong it may be, on the strength of some particular rule, a given act may be judged as not wrong or wholly wrong or "really" wrong when all relevant moral considerations are admitted. This is the point, for instance, of the exchange between Cephalus and Socrates, in the First Book of the *Republic*. It signifies the eligibility of cases subsumed under a given rule to be subsumed as well under more comprehensive rules.

So "Lying is wrong," taken as a tautology, is incapable of being disputed. But, as a tautology, it is empty and even superfluous as far as the principal moral issues are concerned. One needs to know the criteria by which to judge an action to be a case of lying and the justification for construing it as morally reprehensible or blameworthy. The statements of these are not tautologies, are open in fact to dispute, revision, and even rejection. The tautological rule itself may, conceivably, serve to reinforce rhetorically the relevance of such criteria and such justification. Or, it may serve to draw attention to an obligation to adhere to such criteria. Or, it may serve loosely to collect memorable and admissible cases of lying by which to guide the judgment of new cases. But these are all quite subsidiary roles.

We may also usefully contrast tautological rules like "Lying is wrong" with such non-tautological rules as, "One ought to contribute to the happiness of others" and also with such rather special tautological rules as, "One ought to do what is right," "One ought to act ethically," "The greater good ought to be preferred to the lesser good." Rules like "Lying is wrong" demand explication but no justification, since they are tautologies; on the other hand, as tautologies, they are vacuous and the question of justification arises respecting whatever may be taken to be the positive content of the rule. But non-tautological rules demand justification and this, as we have already seen, is extremely difficult to provide in any way that may fairly count as proof or confirmation. Still again, although we may dispute that lying is wrong—in the sense in which we may say that lying is not always wrong (may be justified)—no similar challenge may be made against rules like, "One ought to do what is right." These are the most comprehensive (and, correspondingly, most vacant) moral rules possible: they neither require justification nor are they conditional rules in the sense in which "Lying is wrong" is. But to know what satisfies them is to know the whole of morality!

Consider, now, that someone has lied. In so far as he has, he has acted wrongly. But the question is, was it really wrong to lie *under the circumstances?* Someone might claim (a likely possibility) that lying is wrong, except to save a life. In effect, he would have formulated a more comprehensive rule than "Lying is wrong" (or, conceivably, a fuller version of the rule intended). It could, however, no longer be readily construed as a tautology. Such a rule requires justification; and, in effect, the justification would show that saving a life by lying is tantamount to "preferring the greater good to the lesser good" or "preferring the lesser evil to the greater evil"—*unless there were additional factors that relevantly bore on the verdict,* in which case, the revised rule would itself be incomplete. In short, the intermediary rule, "Lying is wrong, except to save a life" not only requires justification itself, but it may also be open to exception; for instance, it may be perfectly reasonable to claim that "saving a life by lying is not always right." Hence, nothing is gained by such intermediary rules.

The rules that appear in tautological form, then, can always be reformulated non-tautologically; and, in that form, they all require justification and are all, if valid, conditionally valid in the sense already supplied. Only certain rules may be said not to require justification—for instance, "The greater good ought to be preferred to the lesser good"; but the reason is that such rules are not only tautological but signify the unconditional preferability of overriding moral values (whatever they may be). As such, they are entirely vacuous. Alternatively put, they are merely the empty, global formulas for whatever specific rules and values the partisans of any eligible metamoral principle may provide. *What* the greater good, the unavoidable duty, the supremely right act are, are precisely the counters in dispute among metamoral theorists. The result is that, under the condition that cognitivism and essentialism are indefensible, it is not possible to enumerate particular, piecemeal judgments or moral rules as clearly valid independently of the provision of some metamoral principle concerned to specify the overriding values of human life. Act- and rule-utilitarianism cannot be satisfactorily distinguished (nor, their deontological counterparts); would-be moral rules are necessarily conditional and we cannot possibly formulate all of the relevant considerations on which we render moral verdicts—other than merely on *prima facie* grounds or in accord with some *ceteris paribus* clause; and the very nature of judgments and rules is such that, both with respect to the substance of their conditional claims and with respect to a global assessment of their *prima facie* merit, ulterior questions of justification arise. Hence, granting the features of judgments, rules, and metamoral convictions already noted, that alone provide a body of initial data about which to theorize, as well as the considerable divergence of practices and convictions among human societies (whether compared synchronically or diachronically), it is clear that moral theory cannot proceed in any more plausible way than to construct comprehensive accounts of the moral life of man that are at once internally coherent, responsive to the large conceptual difficulties that other alternatives have failed to heed, relatively non-arbitrary, and relatively explicit about the nature and extent of their particular accommodation of the provisional data with which all competing theories must begin.

Unless moral convictions are somehow self-certifying, it is hopeless to defend any particular doctrine (*pace* Aristotle, Mill, Ross, and their successors) by appealing to the mature moral conscience, to those who love their fellow men, to the sensitive souls of each of us, who know in our hearts what we believe to be good and right.

CHAPTER 9

The Confirmation of Metamoral Theories

THE DIFFICULTIES confronting all metamoral theories may be specified, conveniently and strategically, by attempting a defense of the principle of ethical egoism. Egoism is a much-maligned and neglected doctrine respecting the justification of one's conduct. By various strategies, it is alleged to fall outside the pale of ethically relevant theories (though what the defining conditions of admissible theories might be is often unmentioned or, if mentioned, indecisive or prejudicial);[1] it is also sometimes thought to be inherently self-defeating or self-contradictory since the rational egoist cannot promote his doctrine among other men (though why he must or ought to do so or why the defensibility of egoism needs to be taken up only by egoists is ignored).[2] The point of exploring the tenability of egoism, apart from its intrinsic interest, lies in the quite instructive light it casts on the proposal of any putatively supreme justificatory principle of conduct. This alone makes it rather surprising that egoism has not been more attractive as a topic of controversy than the literature indicates, for it is by no means without charm or force or subtlety.

Traditionally, the particular bite of egoism has been assigned to its possible parity with utilitarianism: the argument, more or less as Henry Sidgwick has noted, lies with there being, for an hedonic criterion of value or for any comparable criterion (that might serve utilitarianism), an egoistic twin of any universalistic thesis. If this be admitted, the question immediately arises as to the basis on which to prefer the universalistic version (utilitarianism) to the egoistic version. It is obvious that, if egoism is either inadmissible on some technicality or incoherent or self-defeating, utilitarians are freed from the responsibility of demonstrating the superiority of their principle over some egoistic twin. Another alternative, the one adopted by Sidgwick himself and, generally speaking, by laissez-faire theorists is that egoism and utilitarianism happily come to the same thing. In our own time, this is bound to appear merely naïve; consequently, short of ruling egoism out for one reason or another, the question posed remains.

Now, an egoistic *element* can be shown plausibly to be an element of any tenable utilitarianism, just as a deontological *element* can be shown to be an element of any tenable utilitarianism. Whether this means that utilitarianism is hopelessly inadequate as a candidate for the supreme justificatory principle of conduct pretty well depends on what is admitted to be the sense of the term. If, by strict utilitarianism, one means the thesis (in any of its versions) that what is morally right is what promotes the greatest good for all (where 'greatest' and 'all' are merely calculative terms, and 'good' designates some quality that lends itself to relevant calculation), then indeed if an egoistic element be acknowledged, the utilitarian principle will thereby be admitted to be inherently inadequate. If, on this reading, utilitarian calculation may, in principle, admit that egoistic preferences do, at times, outrank utilitarian ends, then of course one cannot consistently subscribe to the utilitarian principle as the supreme principle of morality. Consider, in this connection, that if the good produced by one's act be considerable and equal, addressed to oneself or another, and if the loss of value in not acting is similarly considerable and equal, and if the act cannot be performed for both oneself and another, it is not obviously unreasonable that one should prefer to perform the act in question for oneself rather than for another:

on utilitarian grounds, on the hypothesis, there is no basis for preferring the one over the other—the matter is ethically indifferent; but on egoistic grounds, the matter is readily settled. Consider also that if the good produced by one's act be considerable and unequal when addressed to oneself or another, and if the loss of value in not acting be considerable and unequal, and if the good that would be produced for another is slightly greater than the good that would be produced for oneself, and if the loss of value suffered by another would be slightly greater than the loss of value that would be suffered by oneself, and if the act cannot be performed for both oneself and another, it would still not be obviously unreasonable to act in one's own interest rather than to maximize goodness. Of course, a strict utilitarian of the stripe already defined will deny this, but the matter is arguable and it is not clear that it can be settled by an appeal, except viciously, to what may be supposed to be best under the circumstances. If these counterinstances stand, they entail either that some ethically relevant choices are decidable only on non-utilitarian grounds without positively violating the utilitarian principle or that some ethically relevant choices are decidable only on non-utilitarian grounds with respect to which, precisely, utilitarian considerations are either violated or superseded. In either case, utilitarianism will prove to be inadequate as the supreme principle of conduct. All the more reason, then, for considering whether egoism might not be a strong candidate for such a supreme principle.

It can also be shown quite simply that a parallel problem for utilitarianism arises *vis-à-vis* a deontological element. Consider that one's acting in alternative ways produces two considerable and equal lots of good and that either alternative produces considerable and equal lots of losses of value, that the alternatives are exclusive, and that the distribution of good and loss is relatively equal on one alternative and is substantially unequal on the other. It may, not unreasonably, be argued that the alternative involving equal distribution is *prima facie* morally preferable to the other. But then, once again, a matter that would be indifferent on utilitarian grounds (as interpreted) would not be indifferent on deontological grounds and we should once again find it difficult to decide, except viciously, which alternative was morally more tenable. Alternatively, a comparable choice may arise where the utility of one alternative is slightly greater than that of the other although at the cost of considerable inequalities in the distribution of good and the loss of good. Under such circumstances, again, it seems not unreasonable to argue for the equitable distribution in the face of an over-all loss of utility. But then, of course, we should be faced with deontological counterparts of the dilemmas posed by egoism. Short of a dogmatic rejection of such cases, we should find ourselves stalemated respecting the supreme principle of conduct. Also, it should be noted, some utilitarians would be willing to absorb either egoistic or deontological elements within their doctrine, though to the extent to which they would do so, they risk obscuring the lines of battle between alternative candidates for the supreme principle. Thus, for instance, one recent utilitarian declares that "considerations of equal distribution are central to the whole conception of utilitarianism." [3] But this is simply to ignore possible discrepancies between maximal and equitably distributed utility; or, if it is willingly countenanced, the definition of utilitarianism will require conditions imposed on the maximizing of strict utility—which seems anomalous. In any case, partisans of the alternative views will have to be met and no conceptual gain will be effected by a mere change of label.[4] The foregoing arguments, of course, presuppose the calculability in some sense of quantities of utility; but this is merely to concede to the utilitarian what is minimally required for his claim to be at all eligible.

Deeper objections to utilitarianism are not difficult to formulate. If the utilitarian objective is to guide rational calculation at all, it must be demonstrable that "the greatest good for all"

or "the greatest good for the greatest number" is actually open
to appropriate calculation. *If* essentialism or at least the thesis
that man has a normative nature which may be assigned to him
on cognitive grounds (a thesis implicit at the very least in Mill)
is repudiated, it will be seen that the prospect of calculability
rests on a number of extremely doubtful or flatly untenable assumptions. For, as soon as that thesis is denied (particularly if
we keep the egoistic and deontological qualifications just considered in mind) it becomes entirely arbitrary to distinguish between the real and apparent goods for "all" (or "of the greatest
number") or to sort out which "goods" sponsored by competing
proposals are the ones to be maximized. But this is not all. For,
on any preference (regardless of its content), it will have to be
supposed by the utilitarian that the goods of all those to be
considered are relatively *compatible,* so that a program of comprehensive planning is even remotely feasible; and it will also
have to be supposed by the utilitarian that the goods of all those
to be considered are relatively similar and predictable, so that a
program of comprehensive planning may be *relevant* and manageable; and it will further have to be supposed by the utilitarian
that the ranking of all such goods exhibits at least the property
of transitivity, so that a program of comprehensive planning
may be rationalized and *calculable.* There is, however, no reason
to think that *if* the values to be realized are to be moral values,
that is, *overriding* values, that any of these conditions can be
met *without the assumption of a normative human nature proper
to man.* Otherwise and more simply put, on the arguments already advanced, the judgment of what values are the prime
values for the lives of individual men cannot but be appreciative
judgments; and if they are, there is—in the face of the historical record—absolutely no reason to suppose that the conditions mentioned, on which utilitarianism depends, can possibly be fulfilled. What we see, then, is that utilitarianism must,
to be credible at all, be committed (however cryptically) to some
normative ideal of human nature—even if pushpin is as good

as poetry, this must be true. Consequently, to be credible, utilitarianism must be untenable. Another, more sympathetic, way of construing that metamoral principle is this: utilitarianism adopts as its objective the presumptive interests of *prudential* agents; these, very probably compatible with the conditions enumerated, are then construed as the *moral* objectives of man. But we have already seen the need for distinguishing between the two and, in particular, the indefensibility of supposing that an agent who prefers to act contrary to these merely presumptive interests is necessarily acting irrationally or non-rationally. The utilitarian, therefore, either on implied cognitivist grounds or on an implicitly normative reading of what it is to be "rational," inevitably confuses the objectives of certain conditional and technical interests with those that concern the overriding values of human existence.

The deontological views that may fairly be said to challenge strict utilitarianism are themselves, it may be noted, open to a counterpart challenge. This may be succinctly shown by examining at least one prominent specimen theory, John Rawls' thesis of justice as fairness (where justice is considered "as a virtue of institutions").[5] Construing justice "as a complex of three ideas: liberty, equality, and reward for contributions to the common advantage," Rawls offers two typical principles for inspection:

> The first principle is that each person participating in a practice, or affected by it, has an equal right to the most extensive liberty compatible with a like liberty for all; and the second is that inequalities are arbitrary unless it is reasonable to expect that they will work out for everyone's advantage and unless the offices to which they attach, or from which they may be gained, are open to all. . . .

The trouble with these principles is symptomatic of all such principles. The first is taken as "containing the principle that similar cases [must] be judged similarly, or if distinctions are made in the handling of cases, there must be some relevant difference between them," a principle that Rawls himself acknowledges "follows from the concept of a judgment of any kind"; it is simply a version of the principle of universalizability or of consistency of usage we have already considered. The second disjunct is entirely vacuous. The principle of liberty holds, Rawls admits, "only *ceteris paribus*" and, explicated (*if* liberty is a good "defined by the pattern of rights and duties"), comes to this: that "if a greater liberty were possible for all without loss or conflict, then it would be irrational to settle on a lesser liberty." But the principle, in this reading, reduces to another tautology of the conditional kind already examined; all similar deontological principles, we may suppose, will similarly require a *ceteris paribus* clause. The second principle is understood as justifying "differences in the benefits and burdens" distributed among a population on the grounds that "an inequality is allowed only if there is reason to believe that the practice with the inequality will work to the advantage of *every* party." But, on *any* reading, this means that the allegedly deontological principle is, in reality, utilitarian in nature. Consequently, deontological principles are typically either vacuous or, when provided content, difficult if not impossible to distinguish from utilitarian principles; and if the latter obtains, they suffer from the inherent weaknesses of utilitarianism itself.

To return to the main thread of the argument, let us grant, then, that there are grounds for supposing that strict utilitarianism must be modified to include not only certain deontological but also certain egoistic elements. The egoist, however, in his turn, may claim that his principle does not stand in need of any such modification in favor of an otherwise competing principle. If so, egoism may very well exhibit a certain elegance and simplicity, and we may well wonder why it is not inherently preferable to utilitarian or deontological alternatives. Let us consider the possibility.

The egoist holds the view that the sole justification for his actions is that they contribute to his own interests, desires, pleasures or the like. Precision is not required here as to whether the egoist is also a hedonist or prefers a conative criterion or the like: the issue is a perfectly general one and holds, *pari passu,* for all criteria otherwise eligible to its universalistic twin. There is, however, an interesting equivocation that arises here. One may complain that the egoist is not advancing a universal principle, in the sense that he is not holding that everyone ought to subscribe to egoism and ought to be equally guided by egoistic considerations (or, that, acting thus, men are acting "rationally" or "rightly" or in accord with what is "good"). If this is true for the egoist, a counterpart complaint may be laid against the utilitarian; for, if utilitarianism is defective, then either a utilitarian is content to provide us with the principle on which he justifies his own conduct (in which case, he is doing no more than the egoist and may, perhaps, be no more than an egoist) or else he is merely advocating that everyone ought to subscribe to the utilitarian principle (in which case, he has yet to provide a suitable justification). In a word, unless one can demonstrate that principles like the utilitarian or egoistic or deonotological are somehow true, on independent grounds (in which case, one may properly and neutrally claim that one ought to subscribe to the true principle of morality), we are confronted merely with the partisans of this or that principle and asked to consider their relative merits without regard to the question whether any one of them is straightforwardly true at all. It then becomes entirely irrelevant—apart from considerations of consistency—whether one advocates his preferred principle to the whole world or not. But this is an embarrassment, given the heat with which the relevant controversies have been waged.

On the other hand, the *objective* of the egoist is, indeed, his exclusive well-being whereas that of the utilitarian is the well-being of all—in this sense, then, a universalized objective. On this interpretation, the charge is true enough but seemingly question-begging, since this is precisely to rule out, at the very outset, the egoistic alternative (an alternative regarding over-riding values) and, apparently, to vindicate utilitarianism with-out a contest. The objection *may* stand, but it is obviously in need of supporting arguments; that is, the egoist's being occu-pied only with his own well-being may violate other (non-question-begging) conditions that defensible ethical principles may be expected to meet. The issue remains, what are these conditions? It may be emphasized, also, that the egoistic prin-ciple *is* actually universalizable in the further sense that every-one could, logically, subscribe to it just as easily as to the utili-tarian principle. Also, the egoist is able to hold that, *if* his prin-ciple is true, then everyone ought to subscribe to it (if they are rational)—though in saying this, he need not advocate it and may, as a rational agent, even hope that others will not subscribe to it. Consequently, short of establishing that one or the other candidate principle is true with respect to the moral domain, the only objection to egoism appears (thus far) to be that the egoist is prepared to justify his conduct solely on the grounds of advancing and maximizing his own well-being— that is to say, he is criticized merely for holding the principle he holds.

Now, the ultimate justification the egoist is prepared to offer is that he is uniquely himself, that what suits *him* justifies his conduct since no one else is, *ex hypothesi,* sufficiently like him (being different from him) to extend the justification to such another in suitably similar circumstances. Hence, the egoist may well claim to do as he pleases and on rational grounds; if, *per impossibile,* another were sufficiently like him, he would be obliged, on grounds of consistency, to regard as justified the other's behavior in like circumstances. In that case, he would, of course, fail to be an egoist, since he should then have failed to *justify* his exclusive concern with himself, however exclusive his actual concern may be. This suggests that we look more closely at the egoist's claim of uniqueness.

If one could show that all referring expressions could be

eliminated and that such paraphrastic programs as Russell proposes in his Theory of Definite Descriptions or as Quine proposes in his attempted elimination of proper names were feasible,[6] then, interestingly enough, the egoist would be easily defeated. For, if individuals were uniquely singled out by some set of indefinite descriptions and the like, the egoist would mean by saying, "Because I'm me" that he justifies his conduct on the grounds of possessing this or that attribute. But then, for any given attribute, accepting the doctrine of the "divided reference" of predicates,[7] the egoist would be bound to entertain a non-exclusive justification of his conduct, since another might, logically, possess just that attribute (even if it is an exclusive attribute like that of being the tallest man in the world); also, should he happen to possess some attribute uniquely, it would still be necessary for him to show that the attribute singled out was *relevant* in justifying conduct in any sense at all. For instance, if our egoist were indeed the only man with nine toes on his right foot, it would normally be beside the point to mention this in defense of any particular action and it would certainly be a bore to have it offered as a justification for every action he performs. On the other hand, programs such as Russell and Quine have proposed are by no means obviously feasible; the egoist is not, therefore, bound to subscribe to them and may well wish to justify his conduct in terms of *his* career, *his* interests, *his* pleasures. On that basis, he could, trivially, universalize his maxims, secure in the knowledge that they apply uniquely to him. Also, as we have seen, utilitarianism itself appears to require an egoistic element at least; but if so, some provision must be made for just the sort of consideration the egoist wishes to elevate to a supreme principle of conduct. Also, the egoist would never be obliged to face a challenge to the exclusiveness of his reasons for acting this way or that and, if there were *any* relevant reasons he might advance, they would all be selected from the set of reasons exclusively available to him. The only criticism that can be leveled against him, it seems, is that his reasons, curiously, will all be degenerate—that is, logically degenerate—since they will never really depend on this or that attribute but only on *his* possessing this or that attribute. As far as I can see, the egoist may be as fickle and changeable as he likes and still be said to act on rational grounds: he does what he pleases, but there may be no other significant regularities that may be singled out. We are, then, pretty well reduced to being spectators of the egoist's life, since as long as he is consistent, there are no disputes possible with him, *on his grounds.*

Here, it seems, a clue suggests itself regarding the limitations of egoism. For, given the egoistic principle, there is no use (except, perhaps, a redundant one or a rhetorical one) for such terms as 'right,' 'wrong,' 'ought,' 'obligatory,' 'forbidden,' 'duty,' 'rights,' 'just,' and the like. The egoist is solely occupied with what, on his thesis, is good or bad. An interesting parallel may be mentioned here: Kant remarks that beings with "holy wills" cannot properly be said to be bound by duties, since such wills never deviate from willing what reason takes to be morally right; only imperfect beings, whose inclinations may go contrary to what reason tells them is morally right, can properly be said to have duties. By contrast, an egoist cannot consistently admit that he has duties because he cannot consistently admit any justificatory considerations that do not spring from his own interests (and, since rules are, for him, predictive only, rule-egoism must reduce to act-egoism). Consequently, an egoist simply does not share any of the usual issues debatable by utilitarians or deontologists. For, not only is his objective his exclusive well-being, but his reasons also are exclusive. It is, however, logically impossible to admit rights, duties, and the like without admitting that the justifying reasons for actions relative to these are, if valid, valid for like persons in like circumstances; that is, the very admission of questions of what is right or obligatory excludes the egoist from the debate, just as the adoption of egoism precludes such questions from arising. This,

I believe, lies at the heart of the charge that egoism is not an ethically eligible position.[8] The trouble is, once again, that the consistent egoist will merely maintain that, with his view, there are no independent matters of obligations, rights, etc. We are, therefore, driven back to our stalemate. Alternatively put, the limitations of egoism are not, it would appear, either moral or logical; they are practical rather, in the sense that the disputes of moral partisans predictably concern precisely those issues that egoism rules out of court. And this means that it is not the tenability, but the relevance, of the doctrine *vis-à-vis* the dominant issues, that will come under fire. At best, however, this is not even remotely decisive; and at worst, it is itself contingent on the stability of all those social influences that make of egoism a marginal theory. But the core difficulty of egoism must still be admitted, that is, that it makes *no* provision whatsoever for the debate of *public moral* policies as such, for it does not consider any recognizable attribute of any policy as contributing to a favorable appraisal (except in terms of an exclusive, personal interest).

Let me recapitulate, then, the main lines of the argument. The large alternative theories I am speaking about—egoism, utilitarianism, deontology—that I call "metamoral" theories, I have distinguished from so-called "metaethical" theories. Metaethical theories are frequently assumed to provide an altogether neutral analysis of key terms and the locutions of ethical discourse employed in the substantive disputes they subtend. But, as we have seen, one's metaethical convictions (as that 'right' is definable in terms of 'good' or that 'right' and 'good' designate independent ethical concepts) are quite naturally affected by substantive convictions—which, therefore, correspond to them and differ significantly from the metaethical views of the partisans of alternative ethical convictions. This is not to say, of course, that there are no relevant differences between metaethical and metamoral views: metaethical theories are theories about ethical discourse; metamoral theories are theories about the supreme principle by which ethical questions are resolved and conduct is ethically judged and guided. It is to say, however, that one cannot identify *in an ethically neutral way* the primary data of the moral domain that *either* metaethical or metamoral theories are designed in their different ways to explicate. The view I wish to put forward, in fact, is just that metamoral theories are not and cannot be *descriptive,* in any relevant sense, of the systematic justificatory features of moral judgments, that they inescapably reform or deform (in an ethically significant sense) the putative data of the moral domain itself and that, consequently, one cannot test such theories by any straightforward consultation of independent and antecedently posited moral data. The difficulty is obvious: the data, which should otherwise include standard and correct moral judgments, are, characteristically, adjusted or reinterpreted to fit the very metamoral theories they are to test; alternatively put, the relevant moral data include, on any generous canvassing, the very fact that human agents subscribe to the various competing metamoral principles.

It is hard to see how it can be denied that rational agents attempt to justify their conduct, alternatively, on utilitarian, deontological, and egoistic grounds, that is, that they—either different agents with respect to the same range of issues or the same agents with respect to different issues—are convinced that reasons of the relevant sorts are at least admissible. But if these practices be entered as part of the primary data which ethical theories of any sort are concerned to explicate, then, obviously, metaethical theories are bound to be affected by differences in substantive ethical convictions: a utilitarian and a deontologist will not only be unable to agree about the description of the conceptual relationship between 'good' and 'right' but they will not, in all fairness, be able to see their opponent's view vindicated by an appeal to the data of the moral domain. Similarly, if the primary data of the moral domain include justificatory appeals to utilitarian, deontological, and egoistic principles (and possibly others), then the prospect of vindicating, in any straightforward way, such principles as the supreme principle for justifying conduct is clearly hopeless. The difficulty, as has been suggested, is that we simply have no way of demarcating the settled data of the moral domain that is clearly neutral and acceptable to the partisans of competing metaethical and metamoral theories. But if this is so, then it is logically impossible to press the relevant disputes in the direction of the truth, and the competing views themselves threaten to reduce to rhetorical maneuvers.

Dispute, of course, is not reduced to rhetoric, but it is, I believe, quite a bit weaker logically than its partisan antagonists are inclined to believe. It is perfectly clear that both metaethical and metamoral theories presuppose some range of moral judgment and moral practice with respect to which they are themselves taken to be confirmed. This, minimally, must include some subset of the actual judgments and practices that a society exhibits and so, eliminates utter arbitrariness. If we can agree that, within limits, a society's judgments will include a core recognizable as relatively ineliminable data for any eligible ethical theory, we will have set at least firm minimal conditions to the testability and defensibility of competing theories. According to this view, for instance, the admission of types of cases like those favoring what I have termed egoistic and deontological elements within utilitarianism is tantamount to the defeat of strict utilitarianism as the supreme metamoral principle. It is obvious also that the detailing of such a core is more likely to demonstrate that no particular metamoral principle of the sort considered is adequate than to demonstrate that any such particular principle is adequate; the dilemmas that have been mentioned for utilitarianism more convincingly undermine that doctrine than they establish either egoism or deontology. Also, the identification of a minimal core of moral data that metaethical and metamoral theories explicate must be admitted to be, at best, somewhat relativized; for, if our foregoing argument respecting egoism holds, we can hardly expect that egoistic, utilitarian, and deontological theories *could* admit the same data with respect, say, to the practice of punishment. This, of course, suggests a counter-strategy: disputes between competing meta-moral theories will be pursued relative to the data admitted; *if* the question concerns, precisely, the adequacy of competing doc-trines to accommodate *morally admissible* punishment, egoism will prove to be flatly indefensible and irrelevant.

There is, admittedly, the risk of tendentiousness here, in the concession of initial data; but it cannot be avoided altogether, since *some* range of data must be acknowledged as that which the competing metamoral theories are concerned to explicate. Clearly, viable metamoral debate will have to be occupied with the reasons for which this or that range of questions or this or that range of judgments ought to be recognized as belonging to the core data themselves—where, that is, the issue is *not* to be construed as itself a moral or metamoral issue. An egoism that rules out punishment or duties respecting promise-keeping and contracts as relevant moral questions *simply because* their admission is incompatible with the egoistic principle adopted metamorally is, to that extent, relatively arbitrary and uninter-esting—but I cannot see how it can be shown, for that reason merely, to be a false principle. This is, in fact, the chief objec-tion to egoism, and it clarifies considerably the nature of what I am calling metamoral debates. Such debates, to be at all sig-nificant, must be addressed to the actual practices and relation-ships that obtain in a given society; but to reject such debates is not equivalent to holding an indefensible thesis, merely a relatively uninteresting one. Once one admits that metamoral disputes concern putatively overriding values, the importance of this concession cannot be ignored.

If, of course, some form of moral cognitivism could be vindi-cated, the conceptual difficulties of metamoral and metaethical disputes would not arise at all and a relatively clear division could be provided, *for any particular metamoral or metaethical dispute,* between *explanandum* and *explanans.* We can only imitate this practice, borrowed from the sciences, in the moral domain—by relativizing particular debates, by conceding that their force is conditional upon the data competing theories acknowledge, *but* where the data cannot be said to be antecedently and independently established. Under the circumstance, therefore, we cannot provide a full model for the testing of metamoral theories analogous with what obtains in the empirical sciences. The imitation of the latter practice is restricted to what might be regarded as a sort of gentleman's agreement: the admission of standard runs of cases thought not to prejudge as such disagreements as between, say, traditional utilitarians and traditional deontologists. Even here, with shifting substantive convictions influenced by adopting the very metamoral principles in question, the imitation will, inevitably, be an extremely fragile one. And once convictions respecting conduct and the justification of conduct, departing rather liberally from the gentleman's agreement noted, be allowed, the fiction of confirming and disconfirming metamoral theories will become increasingly obvious.

Under these conditions, I am inclined to think that disputes about metamoral principles may be conducted only in a manner reminiscent of the appreciative disputes among connoisseurs of art. What we have before us is not so much a stable collection of undisputed moral judgments and recognizably defensible moral practices, as an evolving tradition of moral debate complete with competing metamoral principles and alternatively systematized fractions of the tradition in terms of such principles. The new metamoral advocate, then, is not so much concerned with a principle in some sense descriptive of the justificatory reasons ultimately offered in the moral domain as he is with a principle by which he may reinterpret appreciatively the entire tradition of morality. Like the connoisseur, he may be expected to be cognizant of the on-going tradition of judgment consistent with all factually relevant information as well as capable of illuminating in a fresh way the conceptual connections between portions and details of an enormous domain. But in doing so, he is obviously not bound by the judgments and doctrines of the past, merely bound to begin with them. I take it, for example, that Jesus thought to reform the morality of the Jews by means of a doctrine that gave a new and altered coherence to that morality: I cannot see that disputes about the tenability of those extremely abstract and attenuated theories I have been calling metamoral are in the least degree of a different sort. I take it, therefore, that each in its own turn becomes a part of the on-going tradition that some new metamoral connoisseur (or reformer) will be bound to accommodate and reinterpret. But if this is so, then some of the most venerable of the disputes of moral philosophy have been, and cannot but have been, seriously misrepresented.

CHAPTER 10

Prudence and Morality

THERE IS A FAIR SENSE in which to challenge conventional morality by way of an attack on moral cognitivism or on the discoverability of natural norms or by way of an exposure of the norm-laden nature of conventional descriptions of distinct kinds of human actions and human roles, offices, functions, relationships or by way of a demonstration of the dependence of would-be moral reforms and the like on alternative ideals of life and appreciative judgments, is to mount too potent an argument. The reason is that, whatever the force of the implied objections, it obviates any consideration of conventional morality from the inside, so to speak. But it is instructive to take note of the conceptual problems that arise within the context of distinctions proper to such a morality; for they themselves lead us to these ulterior issues and thereby confirm the continuity of moral theory and moral practice.

Let us choose, then, as a specimen range of cases, those concerning the taking of a life—which promises to exhibit most perspicuously the systematic features of moral practice. Let me explain. The taking of a life is an action that may be directed against oneself (suicide) or against another (murder); it may be performed by men *qua* men (as in self-defense) or by men *qua* functionaries of one sort or another (as in soldiering in combat); it may be directed against men and (at least) against animals (as in the mistreatment of pets and experimental animals); it is an action one may deliberately aim at or knowingly perform in deliberately aiming at something else that causally entails it; and it is an action that one may perform by way of deliberate commission or by way of negligence and omission (as in careless driving). It may well be that the analysis of the taking of a life requires a more comprehensive network of moral concepts than does any other action; it is certainly a kind of action that calls into consideration all the possible dimensions of moral inquiry.

It is sometimes maintained that the taking of human life—in fact, the taking of any life—is morally reprehensible. But this, as for instance among the Jains, is an extremely hard doctrine, for it denies the bare debatability of relevant appraisals of deliberate action and it precludes justification (as in self-defense) and excuse (as in a crime of passion); maneuvers of just these sorts are, furthermore, normally available in the assessment of other forms of human conduct. Also, it appears to go against the familiar defense that the agent responsible was "acting in the line of duty"—where the sense is that what he did, in taking a human life, was done in fulfilling his duty. There is, of course, an important equivocation lurking here: our agent may have taken a human life, where doing so was itself a proper part of his duty, given the circumstances; or he may have taken a human life, knowingly and thus deliberately, though as an unavoidable result of doing his duty, which, however, cannot have been construed as itself properly requiring the taking of another life. So, for example, a soldier in combat is characteristically said to be performing his duty when, under given circumstances, he deliberately aims at killing the enemy; and a policeman is said to be performing his duty when, under given circumstances, he happens (knowingly) to kill a fugitive he is, as a proper part of his duty, trying to apprehend. Warfare may (arguably) be condemned, therefore, on grounds that preserve the usual arena of justification and excuse. For, it may be held to be wrong to assign one a duty or a right to take another's life in pursuing a war, either because the particular war in question is alleged to be morally unjustified or because it is alleged that no war can be justified or because, even in a just war or a war that is not clearly unjustified, it is alleged to be morally wrong to construe aiming at killing another as itself constituting a proper part of a combatant's duty or right. Parallel distinctions may be formulated for all the varieties of the taking of a life. But all of the alternative strategies, of course, invite appropriate countermoves.

If one insists that, under no circumstances, is it morally admissible that aiming at taking another's life is a proper part of one's duty (or right) *qua* functionary, it must be held that men *qua* men cannot justifiably take another life, cannot deliberately aim at taking another's life. But this is simply the extreme thesis we have already set aside. *If* self-defense, for instance, which concerns men *qua* men and not, or at least not merely, men in this or that role or function, is in principle admissible, then one cannot categorically disallow taking another's life as a proper part of one's or right in a given role or function (for instance, in combat, as a soldier or gladiator). And if, by applying the principle of double effect,[1] it is morally permissible to take another's life when properly aiming at another effect in accord with one's duties or with what is right, knowing that that other action causally entails the taking of life, then, without additional constraints, it is simply a matter of ingenuity (assuming the sincerity of intentions) as to whether the taking of another's life is or is not permissible. One cannot, for instance, aim at killing an enemy soldier without aiming at killing a *man;* no circumscribing of the duties or rights of office or function can eliminate this trivially obvious (but enormously important) causal linkage. And if aiming at incapacitating or overcoming the enemy results, by way of a double effect, in killing the enemy, it inevitably results in killing a *man.* It is clear, therefore, that restrictions of any allegedly desirable sort against the taking of life will, realistically, have to be built into the duties or rights of functionaries and of men *qua* men *and* into the range of tolerance regarding relevant double effects.

The preservation of one's own life is—to put the matter in the least quarrelsome way—at least a presumptive interest of each man, a *prima facie* prudential concern. A rational suicide, therefore, must have repudiated this interest; and a rational agent who aims at taking another's life must have interposed at least morally relevant considerations to justify his action, for to go against the presumptive interests of any agent requires explanation and defense and a matter as decisive for any life as death cannot fail to pit prudential interests and conditional values against one's overriding values.

In this regard, suicide proves to be both simpler and more difficult to assess than taking another's life. For one thing, a man cannot suicide but as a man; there is no sense in which a functionary *qua* functionary can suicide, though a man may well be driven to suicide, because of his handling of his role or function, or he may take his own life, by a double effect, in following his duty (as to avoid capture while spying). But a man may take another's life both as a functionary (as a soldier) and as a man (in self-defense). There is also a further distinction required. A man, we say, may have a duty as well as a right to take another's life, *qua* functionary; but it is debatable whether a man *qua* man can be said to have a duty to take another's life as well as a right. The key here is that it makes no sense to say that a man has a duty or a right *sans phrase* to take another's life. It may be argued that a man has a right, *in self-defense,* to take another's life (either aiming directly at it or in the manner of a known double effect), but it is doubtful that a man can be said to have a duty, *in self-defense,* to take another's life (that is, to aim at it directly). It is only in a special relationship that man *qua* man has even a right to take another's life; else, *qua* functionary, he may have both a right and a duty to aim at taking another's life. And it is only if man *qua* man can be said to have a duty to preserve his own life (the issue of suicide) that it is even possible to consider, in the special context of self-defense and the like, that a man *qua* man may have a *duty* to take another's life. As a functionary or in some special role (as a providing father or as a concerned citizen confronting a ruinous tyrant), a man may be said to have a duty or a right to take the life of another obstructing or endangering a sufficiently important moral engagement; but in such cases, he cannot be said to have the right or duty because he has an independent duty to preserve his own life or because he has a duty or a right *sans phrase* to take another's life; and if it were claimed that he had a duty to preserve his own life, it would be because he had an ulterior duty, as functionary or the like, to perform some other act. The upshot is that one cannot be held to have a duty *sans phrase* to preserve his own life, unless it is possible to defend it on the basis of the determinate natural norms of human life. The prominent thesis that suicide is, as such, morally indefensible is, therefore, either quite arbitrary or conceptually defective; and the thesis that taking the life of another is a man's duty or right *sans phrase* is simply incoherent.

One must be in a special relationship or role to have, under any circumstances, a right or a duty to take another's life; and, in the absence of any defensible duty to preserve one's own life, an explanation of suicide may be given at least in terms of the loss of the presumptive interest of self-preservation. Suicide, therefore, is rather a borderline moral issue; for the rational suicide will have found no overriding moral duties that require his continued life (as a functionary or in special roles) and he will be able to assign no overriding moral values *for* committing suicide (though, of course, he may, as a functionary or in a special role, admit overriding moral reasons for forfeiting or sacrificing his own life—as a contrite murderer facing the prospect of capital punishment or as a patriot laying down his life for his country). Taking another's life, however, is inevitably a moral issue for a rational agent, both because it characteristically arises in the institutionalized setting of roles and functions and assignable rights and duties and because it opposes in the profoundest way possible the presumptive interests of prudential agents. Consequently, moral speculation about suicide must, even initially, be conducted in a more strenuous way than speculation about the taking of another's life; for we may, at least provisionally, fall back upon the established conventions of our society regarding the latter, but we are obliged to defend the prohibition against suicide (or, for that matter, the alleged moral right to suicide) on some doctrine of the natural duties of men to themselves.

An exceptional case is that of euthanasia. A dying or ill or suffering man may be a would-be suicide though incapable of the act. If the defense of suicide is plausible—given no natural obligation *sans phrase* to preserve one's life—then the defense of euthanasia for rational, would-be suicides is greatly facilitated. Under *such* circumstances, the agent either acts as a functionary (for instance, *qua* promisor) or by virtue of a special relationship (for instance, as a member of the family or close friend or trusted physician—as someone, that is, who may be supposed to favor the other's presumptive interests and to know of his desire to die). Otherwise, as with congenital monsters, deformed infants, irrational creatures, incompetents, and the like, the only basis for claiming a right of euthanasia (there is no coherent sense in speaking of a duty) is, precisely, that if suicide is rationally defensible, then the conditions in question could not either promote or support the presumptive interest of self-preservation and a rational agent, *per impossibile,* would prefer suicide under such conditions. The argument for euthanasia, therefore, is conceptually dependent on that for suicide, though, as involving the taking of another's life, it presupposes some special role or office or relationship in terms of which moral justification may be provided. Suicide, on the other hand, has only certain moral aspects—is not essentially a moral issue in the same sense —in that a rational agent must consider whether there are overriding obligations for *preserving* his life. If he thought that suicide was indeed his *supremum bonum,* then—as Kant supposed —his view would be self-contradictory; but the suicide may well be a rational man acting directly with regard only to his presumptive interests and having satisfied himself that no external, overriding obligations obtain. He does not choose suicide to realize his overriding values, but in lacking an interest in self-preservation, he lacks an interest in those possible overriding values that might otherwise concern his own well-being. Only if one supposed that a man had a right to suicide could it be construed as an act defended on moral grounds, but the anomaly remarked would still obtain.

The asymmetry noted is of considerable importance. For, as has been argued, one cannot have a duty or a right *sans phrase* to take another's life and the specification of a duty or right respecting another's life must be made in terms of some relatively formalized role or function or office or relationship. Clearly, then, the strength and appeal of conventional morality depends to a considerable extent on the distinctness and systematic scope of our ways of describing men as functioning in this or that office, role, or relationship and of describing the acts they perform in this or that functionally significant way. A man shoots another man: we say that a soldier, under conditions of combat, is performing his duty in killing the enemy; or we say that a man, in self-defense and with his own life in peril, protects himself in any way he can. But there are complications that arise.

For one thing, to admit that a man is functioning, in a given situation, in some institutionally recognizable way is not in itself equivalent to accepting conventionally imposed norms for assessing such actions. Imagine, for instance (as in the Nuremburg Trials, or, more recently, as alleged, in Vietnam), that a combat soldier following military orders takes the lives of some village civilians, including women and children. He assumes that he is acting in accord with his duty and is, therefore, not guilty of murder. It is quite possible both that he *is* acting in accord with his duty as stipulated and that the moral sensibilities of his society change so that the limits of his proper duty are altered or more fully defined, to disallow taking the lives of "innocent" people (that is, minimally, non-combatants), whether or not he is acting under military orders. The moral reform and revision of the duties and rights of a man *qua* functionary (or of a man *qua* man, in special circumstances) is entirely eligible.

A second consideration is this. Social changes may be so extraordinary that the patchwork revision of conventional codes long operative within an established society may prove extremely difficult if not impossible to manage. Imagine (as is actually the case) that the signatories of the Geneva Protocol[2] on warfare and other nations said to subscribe to its terms are obliged to examine the compatibility of the intent and of certain central features of the Protocol and the realities of modern warfare. For example, it now appears to be tactically impossible, with high-altitude bombing, to discriminate between combatants and non-combatants. Consequently, either some radically concessive form of the double effect thesis will have to be invoked (more and more concessive and more and more obviously pointless as a constraint, with increasingly powerful weapons) or else the technology of modern warfare (the various ultimate bombs and chemical and biological warfare) will have to be condemned unconditionally. The dilemma facing us here is obvious: on the one hand, if war is legitimate at all, then victory is its presumptive goal and no reduction in power relative to that goal is rational; and on the other, if the risk and threat of war cannot be effectively controlled by the would-be moral agents who condemn it, then, given their own presumptive interests, they cannot rationally condemn it unconditionally. If, say, the United States and the Soviet Union both condemn the testing and the use of nuclear weapons and if, say, mainland China refuses to do so, then it is difficult to see how either the United States or the Soviet Union can escape entertaining the *moral* defensibility of perfecting and using the most powerful weapons imaginable against one another or against any new force capable of mounting a relevant threat. But to say that they subscribe to a *conditional* ban on nuclear weapons and the like is to say that the ultimate decision is a prudential rather than a moral one; for, it concedes in principle that, under likely circumstances, it would not be immoral to risk the use of ultimate weapons or weapons that cannot but fail, in a radical sense, to distinguish between combatants and non-combatants. The point has, just the other day, been confirmed by President Nixon's declaration that the United States will never *initiate* the use of germ warfare. Rationally, no fuller assurance could be given, assuming the legitimacy of war; but, on that assumption, even the statement of this intention—covering as it must prudential considerations—can only be given provisionally. Some version of the doctrine of "clear and present danger" is bound to be held in reserve.

The problem of the morality of warfare is not merely technological but, in a profound sense, social. There is an initial, intuitively plausible view that a functioning combatant may be admitted to have certain rights and duties *qua* functionary, if he confines his actions to what his function requires and allows—in particular, if he aims his actions at enemy combatants only; with this view, technological novelties require a careful scrutiny of relevant double effects, and these (as we have seen) may be restricted, rationally—on the assumption of a legitimate war—in a provisional way only. But the social issue, precisely, concerns the conceptual difficulty of sorting out combatants and non-combatants, enemies properly so-called, neutrals, and allies. We have actually arrived, in our own time, at a point at which such distinctions are genuinely puzzling. For example, is it entirely beyond debate whether factory workers, mothers bearing potential warriors, infants as such warriors, hospital personnel working to patch up a potential enemy, Red Cross personnel providing relief and food to a beleaguered combatant are or are not themselves combatants? The usual conventions are clear, but if the conception of warfare is fairly enlarged so that entire societies fighting possibly for hundreds of years are taken to be the enemy, the distinction between combatant and non-combatant will become increasingly tenuous. Change the context of warfare, construe it in class or racial terms, concede such views as those of Trotsky and Frantz Fanon,[3] and all of the usual well-known conventions respecting warfare will be outmoded at a stroke. Who is the enemy of the proletarian revolutionary or of the black colonial, and who is the enemy even in so-called "wars of national liberation"? In these altered contexts, the very terms of the Geneva Protocol may, not unreasonably, be taken to favor the interests of the established enemy himself, for it recognizes only established national states as relevant agents. In a word, the conceptual difficulty lies with the fact that war has become informal and the distinction between men with special interests and convictions and men as special functionaries has become more tenuous.

The problem goes deeper, for—without at all intending to concede every piece of arbitrary slaughter—conventional justice is always the institution that established powers are prepared to support; and, in our own time, so much of organized violence whether nuclear or conventional is directed against such powers. Would it be murder or warfare if radical Japanese students were to attempt to assassinate a Prime Minister favoring American war policies? Would it be murder or warfare if a North Vietnamese agent were to attempt to assassinate the President of the United States? Would it be murder or warfare if an American extremist, persuaded that "the military-industrial complex" is at war with a developing society that includes an enormous number of Americans as well as Vietnamese (and others) were to attempt to assassinate the President? It is no longer possible, in the face of emergent ideological groupings along such lines, to dismiss such cases out of hand. What is the proper classification (on moral, not juridical, grounds) of an Arab saboteur who attempts to blow up a bus station in Haifa or a U.S. library in Rome? What is the proper classification of a black ambush of Chicago police? The question of war strains our network of moral concepts even more strenuously than does suicide because it is, precisely, directed against the lives of others and (self-defense aside) based on the alleged primacy of certain presumptive interests. Even in the great revolutions—the French and the Russian—the assumption was made that the overriding moral values allegedly served coincided with the prudential interests of the historically "selected" class; nevertheless, the thesis that the dialectical process of history identifies higher and lower moralities is as dubious, conceptually, as evolutionary doctrines of morality (of which it is, perhaps, merely a special instance) or natural law doctrines and the like. We are left, therefore, with clear presumptive interests and debatable and incompatible moral ideologies. How is it possible to defend the taking of life —in the massive doses of past and probably future revolutions— except in terms of one's adherence to relatively plausible (but by no means confirmable) theories of normative human relations and human progress?

And yet, the fundamental objection to murder is that it is the deliberate taking of another life either arbitrarily or primarily for prudential or self-seeking reasons or when usurping legitimate authority authorized to do so. The hangman is not a murderer (which is not to resolve the question of capital punishment), but the man who kills for gain or revenge is the paradigm murderer. The fanatic assassin, we suppose, is a murderer; and yet, with shifting and plural ideologies, the line of division is extraordinarily hard to draw. Genocide, from this point of view, strikes one as murder, on the grounds that no relevant, disputable differences could possibly be identified, through entire populations, along racial, ethnic, religious, or political lines. But the divisions of Nigeria, the Middle East, India, Indonesia—to mention only a few of the relevant, most recent instances— demonstrates that, even here, counter-arguments are not entirely implausible. The trouble, I have already said, is that war has become informal (at the same time that it has become more terrible). And this means that men *qua* men tend *ad hoc* to arrogate to themselves special roles or functions which have not yet hardened (and, in a certain sense, could not harden) into established and legitimized practices. To the extent that these are indeed *ad hoc,* the taking of life is murder; and to the extent that they are legitimized as the historical conditions on which subsequent stable societies critically depend (as in the great revolutions), the taking of life is construed in terms of special roles—the citizen, the visionary reformer, the founder of a society and the armies of specialist warriors who must service the cause. But it is obvious that a clean line cannot be drawn here and will be variously marked, in all sincerity, depending on partisan conviction and even historical fortunes. Still, it is not in the least a conceptually reliable assessment that would make the justification of prospective wholesale slaughter depend on the pious retrospective views of beneficiaries and victims. War, therefore, resembles and may be contrasted with suicide: for, in war, we assume certain (collective) prudential interests to be paramount—whereas, in suicide, the paramount (personal) presumptive interest is just what is lacking; and in war, we construct a plausible moral defense in terms of our ideals and ideologies—whereas, in suicide, we confirm that there are no overriding obligations of a special sort enjoining the preservation of one's life. The conceptual embarrassment posed by both is precisely what, in murder, we condemn—namely, the subversion of moral ends by merely presumptive and self-seeking interests. In suicide, such interests are given up, but it is precisely this that is central; and in war, such interests are characteristically alleged to be coextensive with the overriding values of the community involved. In rational suicide, no moral condemnation seems sufficiently persuasive; and in rational war (apart from self-defense), no moral justification seems sufficiently persuasive. The truth is that, in different ways, moral and prudential interests collide in both.

The *prima facie* reasonableness of war, then, lies in the vision of a better social order; precisely because it tears the fabric of society, it cannot be institutionally justified and whatever justification it has will always, to disinterested parties, appear as the rationalization of presumptive interests. Murder, which might otherwise seem to be war on a personal scale (Hobbes seems almost to have thought so), presupposes some established social order, within which the straightforward equivalence of presumptive and self-seeking interests and overriding values is refused. Here, perhaps, the reasoning may be construed thus: only if a man *qua* man had a right *sans phrase* to take another's life could he be said to have a right, in furthering his own interests, to take another's life; and only if he had a duty to pursue his own interests could he be said to have a duty, in furthering those interests, to take the life of someone judged to be an obstruction. In this sense, pursuing one's interests generally does not confer a special role or function on a man in virtue of which murder may be claimed as a right or a duty. All men are presumed to pursue their interests, and so no moral advantage accrues in doing so.

A number of borderline cases suggest themselves. For one, cannibalism (practiced in order to survive) cannot even begin to be defended except in circumstances of dreadful extremity in which the usual alternatives to the murderous pursuit of one's own interests is at least temporarily impossible. Here, the situation is rather like war, except that bare personal survival in the context of an ineffectual and provisionless society rather than the collective vision of a better society is the spur; for, as in war, every relevant justification will appear to others to be a rationalization only. Here, it may be argued that no one can convincingly arrogate to himself the right (*a fortiori,* the duty) to take another's life, under any circumstances, to serve merely as food. Repugnant as it may be, it is difficult to deny that a would-be defense is somewhat strengthened if all those involved would, given their own interest in survival, agree to participate by lottery or similar practice, under the extraordinary conditions supposed. By this means, the putative right to slaughter another human being for food is mediated at least by a social convention employed for similar, if less extraordinary, impasses. Every justification will, however, as already remarked, seem insufficiently strong. The reason is that the entire force of a morally directed society resists the taking of life for prudential or self-seeking ends (murder) and cannibalism will seem a particularly gruesome form of such prudence. Still, granting the conceptual difficulties posed by suicide and war, the resolution of the issue of cannibalism is not an easy one: I foresee, by a kind of Malthusian projection, that an increase in cannibalism is no more outrageous an expectation for the future than a doomsday war.

The slaughter of animals is another exceptional case. For one thing, man is a carnivore though, conceivably, he need not be. For another, animals (unlike infants) are essentially incapable of being responsible moral agents themselves—there is at least this difference between bare cannibalism and the eating of meat. If it were conceded that men had a right to eat other men, then, universalized, each of us would have to acknowledge that another would have the right to eat him. But this argument is more convincing prudentially and psychologically than morally, as in fact is the argument that we ought not to eat moral agents or creatures of our own species (since, on the other hand and characteristically, we believe we have a right and even a duty to kill others in furthering some allegedly just war). That is, it is extraordinary to hold that men lack a right to practice cannibalism under certain extreme conditions threatening survival, if it is also maintained that they have a right to kill one another in war, where putatively paramount interests are decisive. Cannibalism is characteristically rejected, on moral grounds, because the agent and his victim are both men, of the same species, and because the moral standing of the victim is somehow reduced by being considered merely as food; but if the decisiveness of deliberate killing be fully acknowledged, it is difficult to see that wars fought for territory, power, the furtherance of favored social organization, and the like can be said to fail to reduce (in whatever sense cannibalism is said to) the moral standing of one's victim. Clearly, no one can, convincingly, be said to have a right or a duty to practice cannibalism (under any circumstances);

it is also psychologically and conceptually difficult to suppose that a man, who subscribes to the usual moral constraints against the taking of another's life, could find it defensible to subscribe to cannibalism—though, as with war, self-defense, and even some forms of murder—it is obviously not impossible. War is, in some respects, less puzzling because it is undertaken collectively and in the name of some allegedly just cause; whereas cannibalism (and murder) are undertaken individually for self-interested reasons. The man who supports a war, therefore, is not necessarily thought to be merely self-seeking, whereas the cannibal cannot but be such; on the other hand, the repudiation of cannibalism, under conditions of certain death—unlike cannibalism itself—characteristically takes an approved moral form. The same is true, of course, of the repudiation of war (as by conscientious objection), but the legitimacy of at least some wars is less likely to be disputed than all instances of cannibalism (which cannot fail, therefore, to be linked with murder). But the argument is an uneasy one and, quite frankly, far from decisive.

Arguments for or against the slaughter of animals, by contrast, can proceed only by way of extension: alleged rights of animals (to humane treatment) or duties to animals cannot but be weaker than such claims respecting human beings. If there are no natural rights and duties discoverable for man, there can be none whatsoever for animals; and if they may be assigned men in order to realize some range of the goals of variable communities, they can only be extended (by courtesy) to animals, who lack entirely the relevant capacities of rational agents. The basis for the extension is, obviously, that *some* species are capable of suffering and that all species are forms of life. On the other hand, *given* the history of human societies, certain prudential necessities are very nearly inescapable, in particular, the breeding and the slaughter of animals for food and the use of animals (sufficiently like human beings biochemically) for experimental purposes affecting health and well-being and the like. Given these prudential concerns as relatively unalterable, the prohibition against the taking of animal life can be constrained only by ulterior considerations—as, for instance, the avoidance of deliberate and unnecessary cruelty, the minimizing of suffering, and the like. But this is to condone, precisely, the taking of animal life for food and scientific purposes. In fact, ironically, given prudential realities, respect for human life may, quite arguably, require the systematic and controlled taking of animal life. But it must be admitted that, once the claims of prudential necessity are acknowledged, it becomes increasingly difficult—under conditions of a deteriorating society incapable of providing services and goods—utterly to disqualify, on moral grounds, war, cannibalism, and even murder. A comparable argument, for instance, is bound to be pressed in the future—given inevitable population increases—for the "eugenic" extermination of human groups. On this basis, condemnation of the Nazi slaughter of Jews and Gipsies and the like may not at all touch the principle of such execution, only the arbitrariness and fraud of the relevant rationalizations. There is no question, for instance, that men of allegedly advanced moral sensibilities have already begun to think seriously of the propriety of selecting among new-born or to-be-born infants those who ought or ought not to be permitted to survive. A special version of the same problem, much debated, occurs in the matter of ectopic pregnancy (and similar dilemmas).[4] Again, as in war, no moral justification of eugenic extermination will seem sufficiently convincing, but it will be impossible to reject such practices unconditionally.

These considerations—war, cannibalism, eugenic extermination—primarily concern man *qua* man, not man *qua* functionary. Capital punishment as an institution also belongs to this range, though the work of the hangman and executioner does not. The justification of the hangman's act is assignable to man *qua* functionary; or, so it seems, for if the argument concerning a soldier's taking non-combatants' lives, whether under military orders or not, is valid, then a corresponding charge may be made against the hangman. The upshot is that to call an institution or practice into moral doubt is to refuse to separate the assessment of the practice and acts performed in accord with that practice. But, further, if men *qua* men lack a determinate right or duty to preserve their lives, then capital punishment (however repugnant it may be) does not, as such, obviously violate any fundamental moral injunction; criticism of it must take the form of ulterior objections, for instance, that it does not serve this or that educative or corrective purpose and the like. Correspondingly, the defense of capital punishment will have to rest primarily with prudential considerations; else, as in war, the moral rationalizations offered will be distinctly variable and insufficiently strong for people whose ideal values differ substantially from those put forward in defense.

Capital punishment, being a drastic institution, could not be convincing at all without the claim of substantial counterpart dangers to the very stability (a prudential concern) of a given society. The defense of killing in sport and hunting—whether men or animals—is weaker, therefore, unless (as is not implausible) it is construed in terms of a relevant double effect, for instance in the training of warriors or hunters for survival or in the ritual education of a people (as allegedly, by the bullfight); in that case, however, the essential issue remains untouched. Killing for sport, therefore, is inevitably a weak claim—weaker where men rather than animals are involved, for reasons already given; and, with respect to animals, given a prominent interest on the part of human beings, its defense such as it is, is strengthened only when constrained within putatively acceptable rules of practice. Against men, its justification will seem arbitrary, or worse, indistinguishable from murder—unless, of course, it too is constrained within traditional rules. But again, given no determinate rights or duties *sans phrase* respecting the taking and preservation of life, it is not a practice that can be unconditionally condemned; and societies may well select (and have selected) a warrior ideal for their own.

There remains to be considered only those cases of taking

another's life by way of negligence or omission. It is clear that a man *qua* functionary or in some special role is, characteristically, charged with negligence or omission in the line of duty or in accord with regulations and the like—for instance, a physician careless about his patient or a careless motorist. These are not disputable cases, except in the sense in which the imposed duties and obligations are themselves placed in doubt. But it is quite usual, also, to charge men *qua* men with negligence and omission, particularly in dramatic circumstances, where some relevant intervention might have preserved a life. The extreme thesis, that men have a duty *sans phrase* to try to preserve the lives of others is, as has been said, unconfirmable. On the other hand, there is little question that performing an act that saves another's life is, *pro tanto,* a right act, an act in accord with the usual moral duties and rights acknowledged. It is possible to strengthen the judgment, holding that men in special circumstances—apart from formalized roles and offices—have a duty or ought to preserve or to try to preserve the lives of others. In the absence of a lifeguard, the skilled bather on the beach who fails to heed another swimmer's call for help is often judged to have been negligent or to have omitted to do what he ought to have done or his duty. The affluent and well-fed of the world are often said to be negligent about the starving and suffering millions of the world and to omit their duty with respect to them. But humane as these criticisms may be, their justification depends on the acceptance of privileged visions of the good life and is, in effect, internal to such visions. The commission of the relevant positive acts is, on the whole, easier to assess than their omission; and the description of relevant behavior as acts of omission will, in the absence of institutionalized roles and functions, be disputed—from the vantage of some competing ideology or ideal of life. The actual loss of life cannot be converted into the taking of life by omission, except in terms of some moral theory by which the event is converted into an act;

and we are simply not bound to accept any particular theory of this sort.

These, I believe, are the principal forms in which moral questions respecting the taking of life arise. What emerges, as far as moral theories are concerned, is this: that both moral and prudential objectives must be construed in normative terms and that such objectives, characteristically, collide in the context of conventional morality. If, as I am persuaded, there are no norms to be discovered in nature at large or in human nature in particular, then inter-moral and inter-prudential conflicts and conflicts between moral and prudential interests are, unavoidably, exacerbated by the earnest appreciative preferences and variable ideals of life of the multitude of human agents on the face of the earth. But to seize the inevitability of such strains is to understand at once that rational agents are bound to attempt to construct moral theories on the basis of which they might hope to guide and govern themselves in practice. For, there can be no doubt that the actions and practices of men *qua* men are already theory-laden, whether they will or not; and, given the inherent constraints of rationality, they must, in particular, be informed by moral and prudential theories.

Conclusion

IF, AS IS TRUE, societies are not organisms of any sort (and, therefore, cannot be agents having *interests*, except metaphorically) and if talk of deities and an afterlife is nothing more than a projection of the hopes and fears of men, then the overriding values of human existence concern the exploration and use of the personal lives of each of us. Furthermore, if cognitivism, essentialism, and similar doctrines are untenable, if metamoral theories cannot be vindicated as findings, if the values embedded in all institutionalized communities—obligations, duties, rights, goods, and the like—are only conditionally and provisionally defensible, and if the visions of the normative life of man are themselves the alternative projections of appreciative judgments, then it is quite impossible that anyone can pretend with any justification at all to formulate, as a confirmable truth, what the good life for man is. This may appear to be an entirely negative conclusion. But it signifies, in a more affirmative spirit, that it is *always* arbitrary to impose some vision of the good life upon a community of men.

Now, it is extremely useful to emphasize that this conclusion holds for moral or *overriding* values, that it does not apply in the same way to any of the merely technical, conditional, or prudential objectives of a given community; the trouble is that the latter are far too important ever to appear unmixed by moral considerations. For example, in so far as medical goals of health are relatively institutionalized, competent professionals concern themselves with straightforward findings that may be seen to service the presumptive interests of prudential agents. The conception of health itself is a function of the changing environmental and technological aspects of human existence: given that the physical condition and the setting and skills of man have changed relatively slowly (until quite recently!), medical goals have tended to be relatively constant; but ultimately, medical norms (which can no more be said to be discovered than moral norms) are responsive to the changing expectations of men, and these are conditioned by the alternative visions of the good life that particular men prefer. Consider, for instance, that a chemical "detergent" of some sort may be introduced into the blood stream to eliminate, for all practical purposes, the accumulation of cholesterol and that the treatment is available in sufficient supply (as by shopping at a supermarket) and is so effective that the life expectancy of the average man is most dramatically increased. In that event, what has up to this time been considered a healthy and normal lifespan may, with understandably altered expectations, be construed as relatively deficient and even diseased.[1] The same considerations obtain for all the distinct, prudentially oriented concerns of man—the legal, the political, the economic. What is confusing is that the presumptive interests of prudential agents as well as the implicit or explicit agreements that they reach are, and must be, from a rational point of view, linked to their ulterior convictions regarding overriding values. For various reasons—not the least of which is efficient planning and a partisan favoring of certain values—it is quite characteristically claimed that effecting a given range of man's presumptive interests or a given range of agreed-upon interests (when universalized) *is* tantamount to effecting man's moral interests as well. This, as I have already tried to make clear, is the fundamental conceptual mistake of utilitarian theory.

In so far as the objectives of medicine, law, politics, education, and economics are matters of public policy (to mention the most obvious, relatively formalized, and professionalized sectors of our prudential interest), we are inescapably bound—in any planning whatsoever—to begin with a fair estimate of the range of presumptive values of affected populations; these are further qualified, in an endless variety of ways, by some mode of canvassing more sensitively the shifting interests of culturally and historically specialized societies. The attempt to reform the normative objectives of any of the relatively professionalized disciplines involved cannot possibly escape a conceptual linkage with the preferred overriding values of the critic: the original norms cannot have been discovered, must (minimally) conform to the presumptive values of the race to be at all supported; and the critic, who cannot himself justifiably claim to have discovered a discrepancy between the operative objectives of this or that discipline or institutionalized practice and the true norms of that specialty, must intend his proposed changes to fulfill in some increased measure the vision of a worthwhile life to which he subscribes.

The result is that all of us exert our influence in the public arena in order to adjust the social forces devoted to effecting favored constructions of the prudential objectives of particular communities. That is, because we are interested agents and because our prudential and moral concerns are inextricably bound (at least causally bound) to one another and because judgments regarding overriding values cannot but be appreciative judgments, we cannot but be active partisans in the social setting. Here is to be found the kernel of truth of both the prescriptive and emotive interpretations of moral judgments. We *are* interested in persuading and influencing others and in expressing our own preferences; but to say this is not to speak of the nature of moral judgments as such, but rather of the typical behavior of human agents, given that they cannot merely discover the nature of the good life and that their convictions about it must inform their engagement in whatever comprehensive plans of social organization their own communities undertake. That is, in a word, the public programs of any society radically affect the prospects any particular person may have for realizing his own vision of the good life in any measure at all and, indeed, the vision he is likely to have of the good life itself. This is why his vision is bound to include not merely a projection of some idiosyncratically appealing life but also an account of the organization of a society that will enable, or at least not inhibit, the flourishing of that life. And this is why, also, communities of men, addressing themselves to the resolution of at least their presumptive cares as prudential agents, rally to ideologies, that is, to systematic visions that link their prudential programs to overriding values that may capture their own fellows as partisans. The trouble—as, in effect, the entire foregoing argument has sought to make clear—is that moral ideologies (that may masquerade as political, economic, medical, educational, legal theories and the like) congeal into normative verities and their advocates move to impose some vision of overriding values upon whole communities.[2] The misfortune is that it is altogether possible to succeed in this, although the enterprise is conceptually unsound.

Beyond this, I can only acknowledge my own favored vision of the good life, which, if it ever were to focus the energies of men, would inevitably be recognized as the cliché it is. It is simply this: that public policies of prudence should serve to minimize the disability of any man to pursue whatever life he sincerely takes to embody the overriding values of human existence. In effect, then, the institutions of society should provide as generously as possible for the presumptive needs of men, and yet, at the same time, in as restricted a form as possible in order to allow the fullest play of the alternative visions of the good life that human beings may invent and pursue.

I should also say—to return to the concept of the moral—that it looks very much as if henceforth the pursuit, by any substantial society, of *any* viable moral vision can, realistically, be undertaken only in a planetary or, more precisely, ultra-terrestrial context. The history of moral philosophy (and of moral ideologies, for that matter) has always been dominated by individualistic ideals or ideals formulated in terms of the dialectics of opposing social groups. But it may well be that the ethical visions of the future—assuming the earth has a future—will be discarded as beneath debate if they do not include, centrally, an account of the ethics of the human use of the inanimate and non-human world. Such a discipline—which might be termed moral ecology—would focus not merely on the immediate use of the world for determinate human ends (which is the point of the older doctrines) but also on the long-term use of the world for determinable ends. In this sense, it would, formulating alternative notions of a global and even stellar ecology in equilibrium, come to specify—in terms of the ancient idiom of rights, duties, obligations, justice, and the like—moral appraisals favoring unborn future generations of men or more simply, some relatively total ecology in which men occupy a privileged but limited place. It is, moreover, easy to see that all of the controversies already canvassed may, with very little effort, be resurrected in a context of debate thus altered. Still, it would be an altered context of debate—in my own view, an improved one.

But to urge these things, I must admit, is to announce my own partisan convictions, to solve no burning needs at all, and to say what cannot simply be true or false. It is, I may add, to say as well what cannot be helpfully characterized in terms of any of the competing metamoral theories so dear to philosophical dispute.

Notes

Introduction

1. *Foundations of the Metaphysics of Morals.*
2. Cf. John R. Searle, *Speech Acts* (Cambridge: Cambridge University Press, 1969), Ch. 8.

Chapter 1

1. (Cambridge: Cambridge University Press, 1903)
2. *Language, Truth and Logic* (London: Victor Gollancz, 1948).
3. *Ethics and Language* (New Haven: Yale University Press, 1944); *Facts and Values* (New Haven: Yale University Press, 1963).
4. *The Language of Morals* (Oxford: The Clarendon Press, 1952).
5. *The Critique of Judgment.*
6. *A Treatise on Human Nature.*
7. Cf. J. O. Urmson, "On Grading," *Mind*, LIX (1950), 145–59.
8. Cf. Philippa Foot, "Moral Arguments," *Mind*, LXVII (1958), 502–13, particularly 509.
9. Mrs. Foot does not attend to these additional considerations, but seems rather to think they are relatively fixed unless one rejects "the whole practice of praising and blaming embodied in terms such as 'polite' and 'rude.'"
10. *Loc. cit.*

CHAPTER 2

1. Cf. *The Language of Morals*.
2. "Does Moral Philosophy Rest on a Mistake?" *Mind*, XXI (1912), 487–99.
3. *The Language of Morals*, 142.
4. "Logic and Appreciation," reprinted in William Elton (ed.), *Aesthetics and Language* (Oxford: Basil Blackwell, 1954).
5. *Ethics* (Harmondsworth: Penguin Books, 1954), Ch. 12.
6. "Some Distinctive Features of Arguments Used in Criticism of the Arts," reprinted in William Elton, *loc. cit.*
7. "Critical Communication," *Philosophical Review*, LVIII (1949), 330–44.
8. Cf. Kurt Baier, *The Moral Point of View* (Ithaca: Cornell University Press, 1958), Ch. 12.

CHAPTER 3

1. Cf. Hare, *The Language of Morals*, p. 68; also, Hector-Neri Castañeda, "Imperatives, Decisions, and 'Oughts': A Logico-Metaphysical Investigation," in Hector-Neri Castañeda and George Nakhnikian (eds.), *Morality and the Language of Conduct* (Detroit: Wayne State University Press, 1963).
2. Cf. P. H. Nowell-Smith, *op. cit.*, Ch. 12.
3. Cf. G. H. von Wright, "Deontic Logic," *Logical Studies* (London: Routledge and Kegan Paul, 1957); also, A. R. Anderson and O. K. Moore, "The Formal Analysis of Normative Concepts," *The American Sociological Review*, XXII (1950), 9–17.
4. Cf. A. N. Prior, "Deontic Logic," in Paul Edwards (ed.), *Encyclopedia of Philosophy*, Vol. 4 (New York: The Macmillan Company and The Free Press, 1967).
5. I owe the suggestion of this word to Professor Peter Heath, University of Virginia.
6. *The Language of Morals*, Ch. 11.
7. *A Treatise on Human Nature*, III, i, 1.
8. Cf. Hare, *op. cit.*, Ch. 2.
9. Cf. G. E. M. Anscombe, *Intention* (Oxford: Basil Blackwell, 1957).

CHAPTER 4

1. In *Freedom and Reason* (Oxford: The Clarendon Press, 1963).
2. See *ibid.* 53–54.
3. *Ibid.* 60–61.
4. *Ibid.* 68; also, 82.
5. *Ibid.* 81.
6. *Ibid.* 13.
7. *Ibid.* 53.
8. *Ibid.* 150; cf. also 152–54.
9. *Ibid.* 151.
10. *Ibid.* 5.
11. *Ibid.* 4.
12. *Ibid.* 12. Precisely the same triviality attaches to Henry Sidgwick's so-called principle of justice: cf. *The Methods of Ethics* (7th ed., London: Macmillan & Co., 1907), 379; compare 209. Such principles must be sharply distinguished from substantive ethical principles, such as, for example, is embedded in Marcus Singer's Generalization Argument, which *is* contestable and which depends only trivially on such a principle as Sidgwick's (newly christened "the Generalization Principle"). Cf. Marcus George Singer, *Generalization in Ethics* (New York: Alfred A. Knopf, 1961), Ch. 4.
13. *Ibid.* 13.
14. *Ibid.* 30.
15. *Ibid.* 5.
16. Cf. Singer, *op. cit.* 68.
17. *The Language of Morals*, 89–90.
18. *Ibid.* 36.
19. *Ibid.* 50.
20. *Ibid.* 27.
21. *Speech Acts*, 185.
22. *Ibid.* 185. We have considered the same question in the context of Mrs. Foot's discussion of 'rude.'
23. *Ibid.* 190.
24. *Ibid.* 189.
25. A convenient way of summarizing Searle's mistake is this: he takes promising to be a "speech act," that is, an act that may be

described entirely in linguistic terms; but promising is, more properly, a morally significant act that (normally) is performed by means of speech. The rules governing promises are, therefore, moral rules, though they may concern linguistic utterances.

CHAPTER 5

1. "What Makes Right Acts Right?" in *The Right and the Good* (Oxford: The Clarendon Press, 1930). Further citations from Ross refer to this chapter.
2. Cf. "Extreme and Restricted Utilitarianism," somewhat revised, in Philippa Foot (ed.), *Theories of Ethics* (London: Oxford University Press, 1967).
3. Cf. John R. Searle, *Speech Acts,* 188.
4. Cf. Smart, *op. cit.* 174–75.
5. Cf. Zeno Vendler, "The Grammar of Goodness," in *Linguistics in Philosophy* (Ithaca: Cornell University Press, 1967), for specimen uses.
6. *Thought and Action* (London: Chatto & Windus, 1959), 223. Further references, unless otherwise indicated, are to Ch. 4.
7. *Ibid.* Ch. 1, especially 17.
8. *Philosophical Investigations,* trans. G. E. M. Anscombe (Oxford: Basil Blackwell, 1953), I, paragraph 122.
9. *Loc. cit.* Further citations from Vendler are from this paper.

CHAPTER 6

1. The latter thesis appears, as we have seen, to be championed by such writers as John Searle, Philippa Foot, and Zeno Vendler. We shall consider, below, one of the most comprehensive doctrines of this sort, that of Eric D'Arcy.
2. Cf. Stephen Toulmin, *The Place of Reason in Ethics* (Cambridge: Cambridge University Press, 1950); also, R. M. Hare, *The Language of Morals.*
3. Cf. Henry Sidgwick, *The Methods of Ethics.*
4. Cf. P. F. Strawson, "Ethical Intuitionism," *Philosophy,* XXIV, (1949), 347–57.
5. H. A. Prichard, for instance, says that "the appreciation of an

obligation is, of course, only possible for a developed moral being and that different degrees of development are possible," in "Does Moral Philosophy Rest upon a Mistake?" *loc. cit.,* 487–99, n. 7.

6. Cf. William Frankena, "The Naturalistic Fallacy," *Mind,* XLVIII (1939), 103–14.

7. Cf. Paul Ziff, "The Word 'Good,' " in *Semantic Analysis* (Ithaca: Cornell University Press, 1960).

8. Cf. Zeno Vendler, "The Grammar of Goodness," *loc. cit.*

9. Cf. for instance Kurt Baier, *The Moral Point of View,* Ch. 12. Baier actually appears to defend morality on egoistic, essentially Hobbesian, lines.

10. Cf. A. Phillips Griffiths, "Ultimate Moral Principles: Their Justification," in Paul Edwards (ed.), *The Encyclopedia of Philosophy,* Vol. 8 (New York: The Macmillan Company and The Free Press, 1967).

11. Cf. C. L. Stevenson, *Ethics and Language;* also, *Facts and Values.*

12. Matt., 5, 27–28.

13. Cf. Joseph Margolis, *The Language of Art and Art Criticism* (Detroit: Wayne State University Press, 1965), Ch. 6, for an application of the distinction to critical interpretations of works of art.

CHAPTER 7

1. I have attributed doctrines of this sort, for instance, to Searle, Foot, and Vendler.

2. The suggestion is Eric D'Arcy's, in *Human Acts* (Oxford: The Clarendon Press, 1963), 6–7.

3. D'Arcy, of course, sees this.

4. D'Arcy, *op cit.,* 18–19.

5. *Ibid.* 38, 39.

6. *Ibid.* 35.

7. *Ibid.* 37.

8. *Ibid.* 38; italics mine.

9. *Ibid.* 41.

10. *Ibid.* 43.

11. *Ibid.* 44.
12. *Ibid.* 38.
13. "Actions, Reasons and Causes," *Journal of Philosophy,* LX (1963), §ii.
14. *Intention,* (Oxford: Basil Blackwell, 1959), §26.
15. *Ibid.* §5.
16. "Actions, Reasons and Causes," *loc cit.* §iii.
17. *Ibid.* §i.
18. I am not, of course, adopting here H. L. A. Hart's ascriptivism; cf. Peter Geach, "Ascriptivism," *Philosophical Review,* LXIX (1960), 221-25.

CHAPTER 8

1. Cf. A. G. N. Flew, *Evolutionary Ethics* (London: Macmillan & Co., 1967).
2. Cf. Roderick Firth, "Ethical Absolutism and the Ideal Observer," *Philosophy and Phenomenological Research,* XII (1952), 317-45; also, Richard B. Brandt, *Ethical Theory* (Englewood Cliffs: Prentice-Hall, 1959), Ch. 7.
3. A recent addition to this popular literature may be mentioned: Robert Ardrey, *The Territorial Imperative* (New York: Atheneum, 1966); cf. also, Joseph Margolis, *Psychotherapy and Morality* (New York: Random House, 1966).
4. J. J. C. Smart declares, in a candid moment, "I wish to repudiate at the outset that milk and water approach which describes itself sometimes as 'investigating what is implicit in the common moral consciousness' and sometimes as 'investigating how people ordinarily talk about morality.' We have only to read the newspaper correspondence about capital punishment or about what should be done with Formosa to realize that the common moral consciousness is in part made up of superstitious elements, *of morally bad elements,* and of logically confused elements. *I address myself to good hearted and benevolent people* and so I hope that if we rid ourselves of the confusion the superstitious and morally bad elements will fall away [my italics] . . . I propose to rely on *my own* moral consciousness and to appeal to *your* moral consciousness and to forget about what people

ordinarily say [sic]," in "Extreme and Restricted Utilitarianism," *Philosophical Quarterly*, VI (1956), 344–54.

5. Cf. *An Introduction to the Principles of Morals and Legislation*, Ch. 1.

6. Ch. 4, 234. Page references are to the text as it appears in *Collected Works of John Stuart Mill*, Vol. X, edited by J. M. Robson (Toronto and London: University of Toronto Press and Routledge & Kegan Paul, 1969).

7. *Ibid.* Ch. 4, 234.

8. *Ibid.* Ch. 5.

9. *Ibid.* Ch. 4, 238–39.

10. *Ibid.* Ch. 4, 235.

11. *Ibid.* Ch. 4, 235.

12. *Ibid.* Ch. 4, 235.

13. *Ibid.* Ch. 5, 240.

14. *Ibid.* Ch. 4, 235.

15. *Ibid.* Ch. 1.

16. *Ibid.* Ch. 3, 229.

17. *Ibid.* Ch. 4, 234.

18. *Ibid.* Ch. 3, 231; italics (and the order of phrasing) mine.

19. *Ibid.* Ch. 3, 230.

20. *Ibid.* Ch. 3.

21. *Ibid.* Ch. 2, 216.

22. *Ibid.* Ch. 2, 213.

23. *Ibid.* Ch. 2, 211.

24. *Ibid.* Ch. 2, 212–13.

25. *Ibid.* Ch. 2, 210.

26. *Ibid.* Ch. 2, 212.

27. *Ibid.* Ch. 2, 212.

28. The point is perceived, for instance, by H. A. Prichard, "Does Moral Philosophy Rest on a Mistake?", *loc. cit.*, 487–99.

29. (Oxford: The Clarendon Press, 1930).

30. Cf. John Rawls, "Two Concepts of Rules," *Philosophical Review*, LXIV (1955), 3–22.

31. *Ibid.* 16.

32. *Op. cit.*

33. Rawls, *op. cit.* 24.

34. *Ibid.* 24.

35. Cf. David Lyons, *Forms and Limits of Utilitarianism* (London: Oxford University Press, 1965).

36. Rawls, *op. cit.* 17.

37. I may add that Rawls' proposal regarding rule-utilitarianism is "bracketed" by him in an important way. He wishes to hold that the utilitarian position may be strengthened by his proposal, not that the view is "completely defensible" (*op. cit.* 24). The fact is that he is primarily interested in the question of justifying a practice and not, narrowly, in a utilitarian defense; cf. John Rawls, "Justice as Fairness," *Philosophical Review*, LXVII (1958), 164–94.

38. This is, of course, a paraphrase of Kant's formulation, in Second Section of the *Foundations of the Metaphysics of Morals*.

CHAPTER 9

1. I should make a particular exception of J. A. Brunton's instructive paper, "Egoism and Morality," *Philosophical Quarterly*, VI (1956), 289–303, in which it is explicitly noted that "what are generally regarded as minimum requirements for a moral system," namely, "overridingness, comprehensiveness, and the acceptance of rules of behavior" are, it may reasonably be argued, fulfilled by egoism.

2. Cf., for instance, B. Medlin, "Ultimate Principles and Ethical Egoism," *Australasian Journal of Philosophy*, XXXV (1957), 111–18.

3. Cf. Jan Narveson, *Morality and Utility* (Baltimore: The Johns Hopkins Press, 1967), 229.

4. I find related and quite similar arguments in Nicholas Rescher, *Distributive Justice* (Indianapolis: Bobbs-Merrill, 1966), Ch. 2.

5. "Justice as Fairness," *loc. cit.*, 164–94.

6. Cf. P. F. Strawson, "On Referring," *Mind*, LIX (1950), 320–35; and Joseph Margolis, "On Names: Sense and Reference," *American Philosophical Quarterly*, V (1968), 206–11.

7. Cf. W. V. Quine, *Word and Object* (Cambridge: M. I. T. Press, 1960).

8. Cf. W. K. Frankena, *Ethics* (Englewood Cliffs: Prentice-Hall, 1963), 16–18.

CHAPTER 10

1. Cr., for example, the article "Double Effect, Principle of," *New Catholic Encyclopedia*, Vol. 4 (New York: McGraw-Hill, 1967), 1020–22.
2. Cf. *Protocol for the Pacific Settlement of International Disputes*, League of Nations Publication C. 606. M. 211. 1924. IX; reprinted, for instance, in Frederick H. Hartmann (ed.), *Basic Documents of International Relations* (New York: McGraw-Hill, 1951).
3. Cf. Frantz Fanon, *The Wretched of the Earth*, trans. Constance Farrington (New York: Grove Press, 1968).
4. Cf. Joseph Fletcher, *Morals and Medicine* (Princeton: Princeton University Press, 1954).

Conclusion

1. Cf. Joseph Margolis, "Illness and Medical Values," *The Philosophy Forum*, VIII (1969), 55–76.
2. Cf. Robert Paul Wolff, "Beyond Tolerance," in Robert Paul Wolff, Barrington Moore, Jr., and Herbert Marcuse, *A Critique of Pure Tolerance* (Boston: Beacon Press, 1965).

Index

acts and actions, 131, 132, 138, 139
  and deeds, 131, 132
  and institutionalized practices, 131–50 *passim*, 189
  causal explanation of, 141–49 *passim*
  consistency of belief and, 37, 44, 53–71 *passim*, 98–102 *passim*
  elision of descriptions of, 134–40, 141, 147
  explanation by reasons of, 141–49 *passim*
  individuation of, 144–48 *passim*
  justifying reasons for, 141–50 *passim*
  moral significance of descriptions of, 131–41 passim, 198, 206
  omission of, 138–39
  redescriptions of, 133, 134
akrasia, 78–79, 83
Anderson, A. R., 214
animals, slaughter and mistreatment of, 189, 202–4 *passim*
Anscombe, G.E.M., 142, 143, 145, 214
appreciation, 23, 41, 45, 47
appreciative judgments, 21–37 *passim*, 82, 83, 210

Ardrey, Robert, 210
Aristotle, 29, 68, 111, 171
ascriptivism, 218
Austin, J. L., 52
Ayer, A. J., 19

Baier, Kurt, 214, 217
Bentham, Jeremy, 153
blame, 99, 100
Brandt, Richard, 218
Brunton, J. A., 220
Butler, Joseph, 161

cannibalism, 201–2, 203
capital punishment, 199, 204, 205
Castañeda, Hector-Neri, 214
Categorical Imperative, 54, 86
censure, 99–101 *passim*
ceteris paribus, 170, 178
character, judgments of, 40–41, 44
classification and goodness, 31–35 *passim*, 104–7, 111
cognitivism, moral, 10–15 *passim*, 55, 56, 73, 88, 104, 115–29 *passim*, 141, 152, 159, 186, 189
commendation, 35, 48–52 *passim*, 80